HISTORY, PEOPLE AND PLACES IN
THE NORTH OF FRANCE

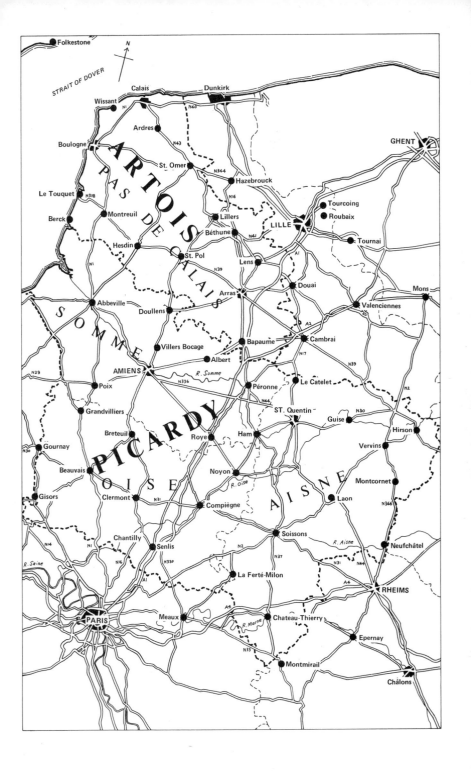

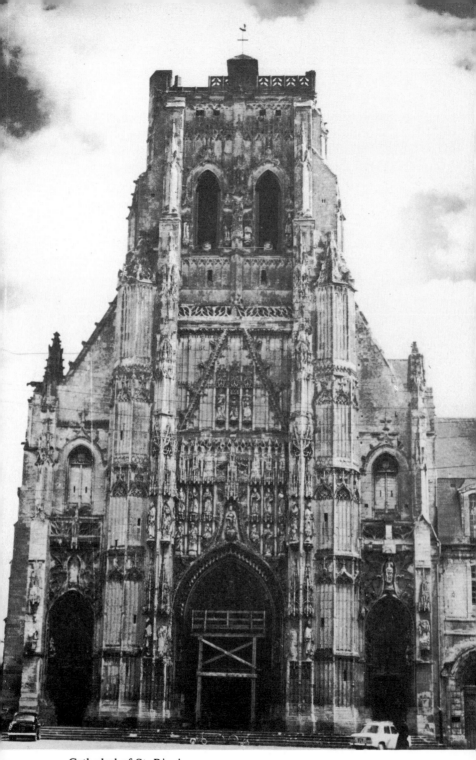

Cathedral of St. Riquier

HISTORY, PEOPLE AND PLACES IN

THE NORTH OF FRANCE

PICARDY AND ARTOIS

Frederick Tingey

SPURBOOKS LIMITED

Published by Spurbooks Limited
6 Parade Court, Bourne End, Buckinghamshire

ISBN 0 904978 27 3

Designed and produced by
Mechanick Exercises, London

Typesetting by Inforum, Portsmouth

Printed in Great Britain by
Tonbridge Printers Limited,
Peach Hall Works, Tonbridge, Kent

CONTENTS

ILLUSTRATIONS

ACKNOWLEDGEMENTS

On my visits to Picardy and Artois to gather the information for this book I have been unstintingly helped by Monsieur Jean Pierre Jacquin and Mademoiselle Anne Marie Goales, secretary general of the Comité Régional de Tourisme de Picardie and of the Office du Tourisme de la Somme respectively. I gladly acknowledge my debt to them. I am also grateful to Mrs Pauline Hallam of the French Government Tourist Office in London for her always ready help.

Some of the photographs on the following pages are reproduced by permission of the local tourist offices of the *départements* of the Somme, Oise and Aisne and of the regional committee for tourism in Picardy.

FGT

1

AN HISTORICAL INTRODUCTION

Less than an hour away across the Channel and therefore feasible even for a weekend visit Picardy and Artois are provinces of great charm, slowly becoming recognised as the only unspoilt country within the London-Amsterdam-Paris triangle. But to the average Briton they remain an unknown quantity, even though he is almost certain to pass through them every time he lands at Calais or Boulogne.

An antique map of France shows the adjoining old provinces occupying most of France north of Paris, leaving only the narrow band of Flanders between them and the Belgian border. Oval-shaped Artois is cradled by the much larger Picardy, which occupies all the coast from above Calais down to Normandy and extends east as far as the vineyards of Champagne. To locate them on the map, look for the *départements* of Pas-de-Calais for Artois and the Somme, and Oise and Aisne for Picardy.

But there is more to Picardy and Artois than unspoilt country, though that is varied enough. East of the breezy seaboard of high chalk cliffs and long stretches of golden sand alternating with modest family resorts, is a region of undulating plateaux cloaked in great forests, vast plains topped by billowing clouds and calm valleys watered by gentle rivers. A region of character, rich in curious customs and traditions, of beautiful Gothic cathedrals and homely churches, proud belfries and monumental town halls, old castles and art treasures of all kinds. Above all, the home of an indomitable people, sincere and given to hospitality, with a stirring history that evokes the sights and sounds of religious fervour, regal pageantry and the clash and cry of battle.

Centred on the historic capital of Amiens, Picardy forms a rectangle some 80 miles long by 120 miles wide. Reduced in size when

Valley of the Marne, Picardy

the map of France was redrawn at the French Revolution, the province once embraced Boulogne and Calais though its boundaries were never clearly defined, except on the southwest, where for centuries the river Bresle has marked the frontier with Normandy. For Picardy always had more a linguistic than a territorial unity, even though the Picard language was at one time the *parler normal* as far north as Lille, as far east as the Meuse. Never a great feudal fief like Artois or Normandy, Picardy long remained a collection of *petits pays* created by the Carolingian kings. The French monarchs who followed them had the formidable task of welding these distinct political entities together while expanding the nation to its natural frontiers. Since the province was the one vulnerable entry into France from England, Flanders and Germany and a vital part of the small area they controlled, no other part of France has suffered as much from devastating wars or been as loyal, a debt the French kings acknowledged by awarding Picardy a unique motto: *Fidelissima picardorum natio*, a nation within a nation, in fact.

Artois, on the other hand, is Flemish as much as French, in its architecture as in the names and dialect of the people. A clockwise tour of the main towns in the province covering an area some 40 miles high by 70 miles wide would take in St Omer, Bethune, Arras, the capital, Bapaume and Hesdin. In the post-Roman days of the 6th and 7th centuries Artois was the province of the great evangelists St Omer and St Vaast, founders of abbeys which were not only centres of knowledge and learning but practical husbandry too, their hard-working monks draining the great gulf which in those times stretched all the way from Calais to St Omer. After the anarchy of Carolingian rule came the birth of the feudal system, when the powerful Count of Flanders held sway over Artois as far south as Montreuil, a bastion of Picardy. Although a vassal of the king of France the Count played a more or less independent role, and over the centuries the history of Artois shifts from one pole to another, from France to the Low Countries and back again.

The province finally became an entity in itself when it was given to Robert, brother of St Louis, in 1237. When the first count died, Robert, a boisterous and likeable character whose face did not fit at court, laid claim as the count's nephew to the wide and fertile fields of Artois. But they passed instead to the count's daughter Mahaut and throughout the reigns of Philippe le Bel and his sons, Robert remained on the outside looking in, frustrated and landless. In 1328 the Capetians finally ran out of direct male heirs and the French peers reluctantly chose Philippe VI of Valois as king, whose first act was to drive Robert into exile. He took refuge in England at the court of Edward III. Edward III was a nephew of the last Capet and unquestionably a French prince, who counterclaimed the throne of France. The Hundred Years' War had begun.

Picardy could not have existed without the Somme, once a majestic waterway into which flowed the lesser rivers of the Rhine and the Thames. Along the valley, where many traces of prehistoric man and animals have been found, the Romans set up their military camps and for a time repelled the barbarians who swept down on them from the Rhine. As early as the 3rd century St Quentin and other holy men wandered about the province preaching Christianity until on the order of a harsh Roman governor or at the hand of an assassin they met a martyr's death. In the uncertainty of the Merovingian and Carolingian periods many abbeys were founded, the monks keeping the light of civilisation burning but also clearing the forests and finding ways to desalinate land newly won from the sea. Meanwhile the towns declined, the economy being almost wholly rural. This left Picardy, the heart of the Frankish kingdom, at the mercy of the

A fortified church at Burelles in the Thierache

Viking invaders, who sailed their *drakkars* up the rivers and destroyed everyone and everything in their path.

While the wanton energies of the feudal lords were being channelled into the Crusades and the towns flourished and were fortified the builders of the small abbey church of Morienval in southern

Picardy created in 1125 the first ogival vaulting, a form of construction that was to revolutionise church building in the religious renaissance that followed. As commerce developed in the towns in the 12th and 13th centuries it created the prosperity that made possible the building of five magnificent cathedrals, each a masterpiece of Gothic art, at Senlis, Noyon, Laon, Beauvais and Amiens, the last the largest of its kind.

The early kings of England forged many links with Picardy when its towns formed part of the dowries of the French princesses they married. These they used to justify their forays into the province and finally their claim to the French throne. It was no accident that the two most decisive battles of the Hundred Years' War, Crécy and Agincourt, were fought in the provinces of Picardy and Artois. Crécy was disastrous enough for the French but the battle of Agincourt virtually wiped out the nobility of the two provinces. On top of that, for 200 years after the battle of Crécy the English occupied Calais, *"a thorn in the side of France"*.

As the Hundred Years' War neared its end Louis XI of France and his adversary, that inconstant ally of the English, Charles the Bold Duke of Burgundy led their armies to and fro across the devastated province, its villages ruined, its fields grown wild and its people dying of hunger and the plague. Yet it was with England at this time that the Picards and the Artesians carried on most of their trade, the one exporting wheat, wine and waide, a plant grown along the Somme from which a blue dye or 'woad' was extracted, the other importing fine English wool for its textile trade.

The death of Charles the Bold at Nancy in 1477 opened the way for Louis XI to unite Picardy with his realm, but Artois, ruled along with Flanders by the duke, was brought into a game of inheritance when it passed on the duke's death to his daughter Marie and from her by marriage to the House of Austria. The newly elected Emperor of Austria was Charles V, who controlled territories that threatened France on every side, though the danger was greatest on the sensitive northern frontier separating Artois from the Low Countries, occupied by Charles' Spanish troops. In 1520, on a meadow near Guines in Western Artois François I of France and Henry VIII of England met on the historic *Field of the Cloth of Gold*, an extravagant display of pomp and wealth. François called the meeting to persuade Henry to join forces with him against his adversary Charles but the English king would have none of it. And from then on until the treaty of the Pyrenees in 1659 Artois was fought over time and again, Charles' Spanish troops razing to the ground any towns in the province that remained loyal to the French crown. Even in 1659 fighting was still going on and not until 1678 were St Omer and Aire, in northern Artois, returned to the French crown.

At least one good thing came out of it. The Spanish nobles who ruled the province for Charles introduced a note of delicacy into the otherwise robust Flemish architectural scene with their beautiful renaissance *bailliages* or guardhouses and other buildings, which still stand in the centre of many Artesian towns.

The teachings of Calvin, a typical Picard, led to the Reformation and the 17th century religious wars of the League, when many of the towns in the two provinces were besieged. The French Revolution a century later did not produce in Picardy the excesses that occurred elsewhere though here, as in other parts of France, the great abbeys were suppressed and their buildings either destroyed or sold as state property. Things were different in Artois, as they were bound to be with the infamous Robespierre having been born in Arras, the capital. His friend the notorious Lebon as mayor was appointed "public accuser" and sent thousands of Artesians to the guillotine.

In 1804, while the ditty that began with "*Merde pour le roi d'Angleterre, qui nous à declaré la guerre*" was going the rounds of the Paris cabarets, Napoleon was assembling 100,000 troops at Boulogne and a vast fleet for his planned invasion of England, a project rendered hopeless when Nelson defeated the French fleet at Trafalgar. "Let us be masters of the Channel for six hours," Napoleon had said, "and we are masters of the world."

Both provinces being on the traditional invasion route from the east it was not surprising that the last shot in the war of 1814 was fired from the walls of Péronne across the waters of the upper Somme. In the Prussian war of 1870 Picardy and Artois suffered again. In 1914 the Germans invaded the provinces from the east and, having occupied Senlis, were almost at the gates of Paris. Even from that distance they were able to terrorise the Parisians when they set up the gigantic cannon "Big Bertha" at Laon in 1918 and fired shells on the capital some 70 miles away. Nearby are the battlefields of the Marne, the Chemin des Dames, the Somme, and, on the heights of Artois, Arras. The battle for the byway of the Chemin des Dames raged for as long as the war lasted. "*A communal grave to bury the dead it cost, would have had to be 20 miles long. They are still there, 300,000 French and German soldiers, locked in an embrace that can never be loosened . . . 300,000 dead, but how many tears?*" Much of eastern Picardy and Artois is marked by memorials. Many of them are to the men of Kitchener's army, remembered still by the poppy that blooms in the cornfields where they fought and died.

The bombs dropped by German aircraft in 1940 which again des-

Cathedral at Laon in the Aisne

troyed much of the ancient heritage of Amiens and Arras formed the tragic prelude to four long years of occupation, when groups of local resistance fighters regularly went out after dark to welcome Britons bringing in supplies and arms. In 1945, well used to replacing what the invader has destroyed, the Picards and the Artesians cleared the rubble and within a few years had rebuilt their villages and towns. Like neighbouring Artois, post-war Picardy found itself increasingly dominated politically and economically by Paris, but the policy of decentralisation introduced in France in recent years has given back to the provinces at least some of their former independence and vitality.

Yet the region remains predominantly rural, a land where the title of "peasant" is still an honourable one. Some of the world's highest yields of wheat are grown on France's biggest acreages on the plateaux of Picardy and Artois. Tenant farmers are most common in this part of France, and the most mechanised, too. At harvest time it is almost like Kansas. Yet elsewhere, as in the water gardens of Amiens and St Omer, cultivation is carried on just as it has been for generations. And the people themselves have been slow to change. Tilling the soil has made them practical, and history has taught them to be philosophical, for it seems that no disaster can break their spirit or disturb for long their inborn *sangfroid*. In the same way that the chalklands of Picardy and Artois are geologically related to the downs of Kent and Sussex facing them across the Channel, so the Picards and the Artesians, reserved, resolute and above all reasonable, have a character and a temperament not unlike that of the British.

*   *   *

Though Picardy and Artois are so close to England the feeling of being plunged into France at its most typical immediately you arrive is stimulating. What makes these provinces so intensely French is their antiquity. Step off the boat at Calais or Boulogne and you tread on soil that was French even before France existed. There is no need to travel any farther to discover the essential France.

But strike out on the *routes nationales* leading from the ports, as many people do on their way to somewhere else, and you could be forgiven for thinking the two provinces had little appeal. It is these main roads, in fact, which have given northern France a bad name. Sticking to the high ground as they do, they give no idea of the beauty of the little valleys, the quiet charm of the modest resorts

20

Saint Nicolas aux Bois in the 'Saint Gobain' Forest

along the coast or the medieval prosperity written all over the gabled squares of the ancient towns they pass by.

While the old costumes are no longer worn and the *veillées* or social evenings have disappeared from the communal life of the villages some events retain a folk-character, and medieval sports like archery and cock-fighting still thrive. Many towns in Artois parade their giants on festival days: Colas and Jacqueline at Arras, Belle Roze at Ardres. Arras, Aire and Boulogne each put on every year a great pilgrimage, colourful and reverent at the same time. A cross of straw still appears on the door of the house where someone has recently died and so do flowers at the foot of the calvary beside the road leading to the cemetery. In many places St Jean fires are lit in late June and they still say prayers at St Valéry for an abundance of fish from the sea and bless cars at Mareuil Caubert to prevent accidents.

Away from the heights of Artois in the east there is water, water everywhere, for fishing, boating, sailing and bathing. The same goes for Picardy. While the resorts along the coast are noted more for their soft sands and bracing air than for sophisticated equipment, many of them have casinos putting on film and stage shows in season, centres organising horse riding in the dunes and beach clubs for children. Land yachts can be hired on the sands of the Somme estuary, and conventional sail-boats elsewhere. Many people come for the fishing alone. Rod and line fishermen on shore or boat catch flat fish, mackerel, herring and ray and when the tide goes out join others in collecting crabs and mussels from the rocks and sands. Wildfowling in the Somme and Authie estuaries is another attraction: over 300 species of migratory birds (some of them protected) visit these areas each year. As well as duck shooting from boats and hides here and along the Somme valley, photo safaris are sometimes arranged. At many places inland and in the extensive forests there are miles of bridle paths, signposted walks and specially-marked circuits for motorists, with parking and picnic areas along them. There are also steam train services for tourists.

Church of Notre-Dame, Airaines

Like the people it sustains, the cuisine of Picardy and Artois is solid and traditional. For generations the ingredients have been confined to what the peasant himself produced and the recipes on which many of the dishes are based have remained unchanged since the Middle Ages. Wholesome yet varied, it is food congenial to Anglo Saxon palates, though some combinations are unusual: duck may come with turnips, rabbit with prunes. Many of the specialities can only be tried in their place of origin, like the grilled or roasted *andouillettes* (spiced veal sausages) of Arras, the *courginoise* or fish soup of Calais, the smoked eels of Péronne, the *poule au hochepot* or casseroled chicken of Beauvais or the *canard en croute* of Amiens, labelled "crusty duck pies" by the pastry shops of London which imported them from the 15th to the 17th centuries. Served at many restaurants in Picardy is the *ficelle picarde*, a pancake wrapped round a ham and mushroom stuffing. Both provinces are rich in both big and small game, from partridge, hare and pheasant to deer and, growing in number, wild boar. The extensive range of patés and terrines includes such rarities as woodcock, eel and *marcassin* or young boar. The rivers abound in trout and pike and along the coast the fine plaice, sole, prawns and shrimps are served within a few hours of being caught. Vegetables, particularly those from the water gardens of Amiens, Péronne and St Omer, are of an astonishing size and quality: those from around Laon include artichokes first planted by order of Charlemagne.

Beer is the drink of Artois and it comes in many varieties, from light and weak to dark and strong. Some champagne is produced along the Marne valley but more popular throughout Picardy is cider, much of it made at home and allowed to mature for several years. An aid to good conversation around the fire on a winter's evening in many Picard homes is the traditional *flipe*, a hot drink made of two parts cider and one part *eau de vie* or apple brandy liberally sweetened with honey.

In their food and drink as in the bountiful land from which it comes, the history of antique France is stored up in Picardy and Artois. So now, assured that we will be well fed, and have plenty to see, let us go there.

2
THE CHANNEL COAST

Below the river Aa marking the old northern frontier of France, a low shore strung with dunes ends on the southwest at Calais, now the biggest town in Artois but once a fishing village at the edge of an estuary that stretched inland as far as St Omer. Part of this gulf has survived in the marshlands behind the dunes, dotted with lakes overlooked by "hides" for wildfowlers and bird watchers, and the remains of Hitler's Atlantic Wall defences. Those near the village of Oye Plage stand back from the shore and were built to look like a church in order to fool Allied airmen.

Standing at the narrowest point in the Channel, Calais is the nearest French port to England, which explains its history in more ways than one. Rebuilt mostly in concrete after being terribly knocked about in the last war, it is still in two distinct parts: the islanded *ville maritime*, the original nucleus of the town, where the fishermen live and the car-ferries tie up, and, across the George V bridge the administrative and shopping quarter dominated by the massive Flemish-style belfry of the town hall. In front of the building is Rodin's famous sculpture of the *Burghers of Calais*, a reminder of one of the most tragic episodes in the town's history.

The Hundred Years' War between England and France had started with the battle of Crecy in 1346. The victorious English army led by Edward III had marched on to besiege the "pirates' nest" of Calais and now, eight months later, the starving Calaisiens were ready to surrender. But on what terms? Mercy would be granted to the garrison and the people, declared Edward, on condition that six leading citizens gave themselves unconditionally into his hands, barefoot in their shirts and with halters round their necks. "*On them*," said the king with bitter hatred, "*I will do my will*." But persuaded by his queen to be merciful he spared the lives of brave Eustache de St

24

Pierre and his five companions though he still drove out the French inhabitants and divided up their property among the new settlers he brought over from England. And for over 200 years Calais and an area some ten miles round the "*Calais Pale*" remained an enclave of the English, "a thorn in the side of France" from which they made regular forays into Picardy and Artois to murder, loot and burn. But it was their turn to be driven out when the French retook the town in 1558.

The town hall stands at one end of the Boulevard Jacquard, the lively main street, named after an iventor who brought such prosperity to Calais. In a park across the road is an old German bunker turned museum that shows how grim life was in Calais under the heel of the Nazis. Virtually all the town's historic buildings were destroyed in the war but off the Rue Royale on the far side of the George V bridge is the old town hall, restored in 1740 but still with its original Tudor belfry, the only one in France. Inside is an historic collection illustrating the love-hate relationship of the English and the French, paintings and watercolours, some by Bonnington and other English artists, and exhibits devoted to lace-making, which was introduced by English craftsmen from Nottingham after the fall of Napoleon in 1816, and mechanised a decade or two later by the French inventor Jacquard. Lace making is still the town's major industry — and probably the only one in France that uses English measurements.

Nearby is the church of Notre Dame, the transept, choir and belfry still as the occupying English built them in the perpendicular style of the 14th century. Nearer the sea is the Place d'Armes centred on the Tour de Guet, a medieval watchtower which until a century or so ago served as a lighthouse. Further on is the more modern lighthouse and across the harbour bridge old Fort Risban that once guarded the entrance to the port. On the mole near the lighthouse is a monument to the Green Jackets regiment who in 1940 made a last-ditch stand against Rommel's 7th Panzer Division to give time for an armada of small boats to take off the French and British soldiers trapped on the beaches at nearby Dunkirk.

Since the action the Royal Green Jackets regiment has worn the battle honour "Calais 1940".

*   *   *

The vast sandy beach adjoining Fort Risban goes on without a break all the way to Cap Blanc Nez, ten miles to the south.

Lace making brought new prosperity to Calais, and the towns fortunes improved further when passenger traffic with England increased in the 19th century. Being situated where it is, the port was bound to have the first regular cross-Channel steamship service which began in 1819. The 27,000 passengers who arrived in 1814 had swollen to 54,000 by 1850 and to 100,000 by 1862. One newcomer in 1815 was Emma Hamilton, Nelson's mistress, who came to escape her creditors and died in abject poverty in the town a few years later. Another, a year later, was the dandy Beau Brummel, the one-time favourite of George IV, who stayed for 14 years living as extravagantly as ever before moving to Caen and ending his days in a lunatic asylum.

In the First World War, still referred to by the people of Picardy and Artois as *La Grande Guerre*, Calais was a major base for the armies of Britain and America and a refuge for those Belgians driven out of their homes by the entrenched Germans. Now it is easily the top passenger port of France.

Calais had been called dull. The area around the *gare maritime*, which for thousands of Britons is instant France, is admittedly not the prettiest of approaches. But once in the animated streets you could well be in any other part of France, so foreign is the atmosphere. Astonishing at those times to think you are only forty minutes from Dover.

On the southwest is ancient Fort Nieulay, restored by the great military architect Vauban in the 17th century, once guardian of the sluice gates which in case of attack could be opened to flood the hinterland, and criss-crossed still by drainage canals and dyke-top roads. It stands beside the main Paris highway but a more interesting way south is on the coast road, in parts a *corniche* giving wide views of land and sea.

To begin with, it bisects the tiny resort of Bleriot Plage, virtually a western suburb of Calais, which takes its name from Louis Bleriot who on the 25th July 1909 became the first man to fly across the Channel. He started from here and half an hour later just managed to retain enough height to land in a hollow in the cliffs of Dover. Further along the flat coastline, the pleasant village of Sangatte was in Roman times the terminus of a highway that ran in an undeviating line from the great star-shaped junction of Therouanne near St Omer. Terminus, too, of the submarine cable to England and of the now-it's-on, now-it's-off Channel Tunnel. Napoleon was the first to plan the tunnel though his aims were not exactly the same as those of the *Entente Cordiale*. The first diggings were started in the 1870's but were soon called off because of English fears of invasion. From the

Ault

top of the Noires Mottes hills, the source of Gallo-Roman finds, there are wide sea views and close by a calvary is the spot from where the Lindemann gun battery blasted at the English coast in 1943.

By the roadside to the south is the statue of the aviator Hubert Latham, the unsuccessful rival of Bleriot, who came down unhurt in the sea, and nonchalantly smoked a cigarette while waiting to be picked up. The coast road climbs a miniature alpine pass to reach Escalles, tucked in a valley whose river has cut a notch in the vertical cliffs of Blanc Nez or White Nose which tower 435ft above the beach. On the headland, near the remains of huge German bunkers built by the Todt organisation with forced French labour, an obelisk commemorates the Anglo-French Dover Patrol, watchmen of the Channel in the Kaiser's war. On most days you can see clearly the white cliffs of Dover. It was from these that England got its alternative Greek name of Albion (white face), to which in times past the French often added the word "perfidious". English Channel, La Manche, Der Kanal, call it what you will, but for the swimmer there is no greater challenge than this stretch of water separating England and France. The first man to try it and succeed was Matthew Webb, who in 1875 took 21 hours 45 minutes. Nowadays record swimmers make the crossing in nine hours or less, though with 400 ships passing through the straits every day the risks are obviously greater.

*   *   *

From Blanc Nez to Gris Nez stretches one of the finest beaches in the whole of France — firm sand that shelves gently into water free from dangerous currents. Midway along it is the small resort of Wissant, on a superb crescent beach sheltered from the east wind. East of Wissant is the village of St Inglevert, on the Nl Paris road, with a church once part of a 12th century pilgrims' hospice and at the crossroads the Cafe de la Muraille, named from the wall that marked the Anglo-French frontier during the English occupation of the Calais pale from the 14th to the 16th century.

Audinghem, beside the sea south of Wissant, is linked by a pretty lane with the lighthouse on Cap Gris Nez, with extraordinary views — when the weather is fine of the English coast 17 miles away. Beyond the fine sandy beaches of the picturesque villages of Audresselles and Ambleteuse is homely Wimereux, with an even better beach loved by generations of Britons. The resort stands at the head of the pretty valley of the same name, famed locally for the cider and

28

crepes (pancakes eaten with a sweet or savoury filling) served at the little inns along its banks.

South is the lively town of Boulogne, once a British colony across the water. In the early 19th century it was also, for a few years at least, a *ville imperiale*, and reminders of Napoleon are everywhere. The château he lived in at Pont de Briques, is on the Paris road to the southeast. You can visit the monument in the valley at Terlincthun, where, on 16 August 1804 he created the first members of the coveted Legion d'Honneur, and the tall column nearby in honour of his *Grande Armee (1804-1814)*, from the top of which you can sometimes see as far as the coast of Sussex and which, they say, can in turn, be seen from the Leas at Folkestone.

From the moment he became emperor Napoleon nurtured the dream of conquering the "damp soil" of England. In 1805, to do just that, he assembled a huge invasion fleet at Boulogne and installed his troops in camps, on the plateau to the north. If the campaign of Austerlitz and Nelson's defeat of the French fleet at Trafalgar forced him to change his plans he certainly gave a new lease of life to Boulogne by, among other things, enlarging the port to take 2,000 ships. After Napoleon's fall the town's growing prosperity attracted many of the English who came to settle in France. But they had been coming long before that.

"*It is well known*," wrote the Suffolk squire Arthur Young, who with typical British phlegm wandered unconcernedly about France in the dangerous days leading up to the French Revolution, "*that this place has long been the resort of great numbers of persons from England, whose misfortune in trade or extravagance in life have made a residence abroad more agreeable than at home.*" The exiles came to Boulogne in even greater numbers in the 19th century, some attracted by the new vogue for sea bathing and the first thermal baths to be built in Europe, some, like others before them, in search of a refuge — which they often failed to find apparently, for so many were detained for debt in the prison in the upper town that the French called the building the Hotel d'Angleterre. But their numbers dwindled as other resorts in France became more fashionable and the last of Boulogne's English residents departed almost half a century ago.

With its bustling waterfront and thriving industry it is difficult to imagine Boulogne as the gay watering place it once was. For a start, the place where Julius Caesar and his legions embarked for their conquest of Britain is now the biggest fishing port of France. The harbour hums with activity and the fishing boats plod out to sea and back again. Inland, along the Liane river, new factories mushroom alongside old timers like Burtons of London and mammoth lorries are loaded up before roaring off on their journey south. Yet families from Paris flock to Boulogne's beach at weekends in summer, only turning their backs on the briny at the stroke of noon to eat hugely and well in the little restaurants tucked away on either side of the steep Grande Rue connecting the lower with the upper town.

Climb up the Grande Rue to the *haute ville*, with its ancient citadel and basilica of Notre Dame ringed by 13th century ramparts, and on the way you pass the municipal museum containing paintings by Sisley, Boucher and Corot, who loved the Boulogne country. Since the 7th century the legend of Notre Dame de Boulogne, honoured with a title in 1478 by Louis XI, has been the centre of a marital cult, and every year at the end of June her statue is carried from the basilica at the head of a solemn and picturesque procession of sailors and girls in traditional costume.

Boulogne suffered greatly in the late War, from the time the swastika was hoisted above the citadel in June 1940, being bombed no less than 400 times before 1945, the *basse ville* where the English used to live sustaining the most damage. Their Edwardian-style hotels and houses have now been replaced by characterless concrete, yet this end of the Grande Rue and its adjoining streets remains the vibrant heart of the town, where the shops are truly sophisticated. A fasinating market is held on Wednesdays and Saturdays in the square facing St Nicolas church, and operas and plays are put on at the municipal theatre, even on Sundays, while the bars stay open until one in the morning.

The top fishing port of France is noted for its seafood and the quality is unbeatable. The offshore boats have landed their catch and the fish market is in full swing by 5 a.m., with mountains of succulent black mussels and rose-red shrimps competing for space with an astonishing variety of fish: mullet, turbot, skate, mackerel, gurnard, sole, bream and John Dory. For seafood at its best seek out one of the smaller restaurants, where a good four-course meal will still cost only half of what it might do in England. After dinner you might round off the evening with a visit to the waterfront casino, to risk a few francs in the gaming rooms, swim in the heated pool or dance the hours away in the slick night club, perhaps finishing up at the nearby Hamiot pub when it opens its doors to the fishermen at 5 am.

I rate Boulogne very highly for a weekend away. The well run Faidherbe or the more amusing Hamiot are cheap and cheerful hotels right at the centre of things. I also like the friendly atmosphere and service in the chic little Metropole in one of the main shopping streets. For serious buying Boulogne has its cut-price Monoprix and

Prisunic supermarkets, of course, and even a huge Champion hyper-market, but for idle window shopping there is nowhere better to roam than in the back streets of the lower town between the water-front and the church of St Nicolas, where they used to say a mass for the conversion of England.

*　　*　　*

East of Boulogne are the Boulonnais hills, a region apart and a charming one at that. A Jurassic outcrop in the chalk plateau of Artois, it has been fashioned by wind and rain into a rolling land-scape of great variety scored by miniature valleys rich in the trout served at the modest inns along their banks. Many of the villages are delightful, such as picturesque Le Waast huddled round its interest-ing old church, or Questrecques, in a scenic setting in the upper Liane valley. One one side of the Liane is the forest of Boulogne, cut into by marked footpaths and clearings furnished with tables and benches for a picnic. On the other is the pretty village and fortified church of Cremarest and the beautiful forest of Desvres. Some of the hills rise up above the others to form vantage points: Mont Eventé at Alincthun close by the St Omer road, or nearer Boulogne Mont Lam-bert (615ft) at Baincthun, are two examples. Place names like these, of Germanic origin, are common to many villages in Artois, suggest-ing a widely dispersed immigration from the east in olden times.

Along the coast south of Boulogne are vast stretches of golden sand backed by a belt of dunes up to a mile wide and 100ft high, an interesting region to explore. This is a shore forever being extended seawards by the easterly drift piling up pebbles at one point and sand at another. These the tides and the currents grind into a fine dust, driven inland by the winter gales to form shifting dunes, their tops smoking in the prevailing wind. As recently as the 18th century they are known to have engulfed whole villages.

By filling up the inlets the sand also created marshes, rendering all the low-lying land subject to floods: at the same time the alluvial soil washed down by the rivers made the marshlands exceptionally fertile once the Picards, a doggedly perservering race, had laboriously learned how to drain them. They also discovered ways to protect the newly-won land from the encroaching sand by consolidating the sea-ward dunes with marram grass and planting pinewoods on those behind to form a bulwark against the sand-laden winds.

Regions won from the sea in this way are the Marquenterre and

31

Aerial view of Le Crotoy

Bas Champs, each about seven miles long by three miles wide. Neither existed when the Romans conquered Gaul and towns now well inland were once thriving seaports. At the southern end of the coast are high cliffs; in line with these are the 'dead' cliffs, still visible on the landward side of the Bas Champs, which mark the former coastline. In both these polder lands, characterised by isolated farms and winding canals, the rich pastures merge into saltings near the sea on which is reared some of the best lamb in France.

In the dunes below Boulogne is the fishing village of Equihen Plage, entirely remodelled after being blown to bits in the war. To the south is an immense stretch of sand, to the north low cliffs and rocks where the locals search for the tasty black mussels. Beyond aristocratic Hardelot, backed by the splendid forest and the heights of Mont St Frieux and Mont Violette is even more elegant Le Touquet, since the turn of the century "*apprecié*," says Michelin, "*de la gentry britannique*," where the huge Westminster with its marbled bathrooms is unquestionably the top hotel. But the hotel with the most cachet in the interwar period and the first in France with every room possessing a bath was the equally large Picardie, where the goings-on were distinctly naughty for the time. Along with other hotels at the resort it became a military hospital in the 1914-18 war. This and the nearness of a big British army base at Etaples saved many a Le Touquet shopkeeper from going bankrupt. The Picardie became the regional headquarters of the German Gestapo until it was pasted by the RAF, and it has long since been pulled down.

Le Touquet is an invention of the British for the British. In the mid 19th century when the area was nothing but arid dunes a few pine trees were planted. They not only grew, they multiplied. In 1882 the first two villas of "Paris-Plage" were built in the forest and like the trees were quickly followed by others ordered through a British company which apparently is still alive and well. In 1912 Le Touquet Paris-Plage became a commune in its own right. Now there are 2,000 villas, most of them white-walled and slate-roofed palatial in the Anglo-Norman style that was all the rage in the 1920's. At the edge of the immense shore along which at low tide the sea retreats to the horizon visitors find an austere Anglican church, two casinos, a park landmarked by a lighthouse, two golf courses, a racecourse and, of course, numerous luxury hotels. There are some fine restaurants, too, the best of which is the Club de la Fôret, one example of their fare being superb lobster grilled with tarragon. The restaurant is patronised mostly by rich eccentrics, people who pay without a murmur the £50 charged for a bottle of Haut-Brion. Le Touquet also has dunes to climb or find a private sun-trap in, sand yachts like "daddy-longlegs" on wheels to sail, horses to ride and a warm salt-water pool on the vast sandy beach to swim in.

In its heyday before and after the 1914-18 war Le Touquet was one of the smartest places anywhere. Once the Prince of Wales had become a regular visitor it was the "in-place" of high London society led by the Queensberrys and the Curzons. It still has a shop called Oxford, a bar labelled Ascot and streets named after Queen Victoria and Edward VII (were they here too?). Many people came for *le sport* (show jumping, hunting, golf, tennis, polo and the like) while others simply wanted to score in the game of social oneupmanship, to escape the stifling morality of puritan England or to gamble in an informal atmosphere. They certainly did not come to meet the French or to get to know France: few if any ever left the resort from the time they arrived until they caught their train or plane back to London. (Yes, Le Touquet has had its own airport since 1929). Times change and Le Touquet is trying to change with them, but I fear it is an anachronism, a sort of garden city ossified by English reserve. For me at any rate it is too formal, too immaculate and too strictly disciplined — even the local *gendarmerie* is made to look like a villa. See it out of season, all shuttered up, and it would seem to have been created wholly for show.

Le Touquet is on the left bank of the Canche estuary. Etaples on the right bank occupies one of the oldest sites in ancient Gaul, a place of some renown in Gallo-Roman times when in 1193 the French king Philippe Augustus made it the base for his northern fleet. It is now a simple fishing port but an active one just the same, with a picturesque fishermen's quarter of low colour-washed houses.

The bridges across the Canche at Etaples were and still are the nearest crossing of the river to the coast. In 1918 German bombers aiming at the big British army base along the north side of the estuary hit the town, killing many local people. But their marksmanship was no worse than that of the Allied airmen who in 1944 aimed for the bridge carrying the Paris-Calais railway across the Canche. Again the town was hit, which explains the newness of many of its buildings. On the western outskirts is the most important British military cemetery on the Continent. The men buried there died of their wounds at a nearby hospital during the 1914-18 war.

Eight miles of firm sand, ideal for taking at speed in a *char à voile* or sand yacht, separate Le Touquet and Berck Plage, founded according to tradition by shipwrecked Norsemen in the 10th century. It was a fishing village during the Hundred Years' War, when it was several times destroyed by the English. Since the drifting sands continually ruined their crops, the villagers had little else to eat but fish. It was still a fishing village in 1836 when Marianne Bouville watched her husband and four children die from cholera. A widow living alone, she earned a little money by looking after the children of the fisherfolk. Taking charge of eight sick children, she let them spend all day and every day on the beach. After a few weeks their health had so improved that she was asked to care for 30 more. This was the humble origin of what is now a sizable health resort which began to take shape with the building in 1861 of a huge hospital, soon joined by sanatoria and childrens' holiday homes. But there is still room for everyone on the vast dune-backed beach, with its bracing ozone-laden air.

*   *   *

Immediately below Berck is the wide bay of the Authie, the haunt of the wildfowlers, bordered by marshes and impossible to reach except

Low tide in the Bay of the Somme

on foot. But a greater attraction for the duck shooter is the estuary of
the Somme, farther south, wider by far and with a richness of fauna
unique in Western Europe, with no less than 300 recorded species of
birds. This immense estuary, with its distant horizons, mobile cloud
formations and shifting sands invaded by the sea at high tide, is
bathed in an intense luminosity which for years has attracted artists
enamoured of its ever-changing variations of light and shade.

35

Along this coast the settlements around the bay of the Somme are the most ancient, appreciated more for their safe beaches than for sophisticated equipment, being only extensions of villages built in recent times in the shelter of the dunes. Since this is a shore where landfalls are easy, invasions from the sea have been frequent. The Marquenterre particularly suffered during the wars with the English and the battles between the French king François I and the Austrian Emperor Charles. But the invaders also came from the north and east and the region was not able to live in peace until the treaty of Aachen in 1668.

South of the Authie estuary is modest Fort Mahon Plage, an off-shoot of Vieux Fort Mahon, from which the beach extends north for several miles. About a mile to the south, Quend Plage is larger and more sophisticated and shaded by mature pine trees. From either resort it is easy to escape into the solitude and silence of the dunes, one of the tallest of which is the Grande Dune northwest of St Quentin en Tourmont, an inland village which has twice been swallowed up by the sand, the church being built on a more easterly site for the third time in 1796. Populated by legions of rabbits, the dunes and fields around the village were owned in the 12th century by the abbey of nearby St Valéry, which had the right to all land won from the sea. As it was the monks who cleared the forests inland and developed the techniques of cultivation, so it was those of St Valéry who devised ways to drain and desalinate the marshlands by the sea. The Picard word for dunes is *crocs* and the hamlet of Le Bout des Crocs near the mouth of the Maye marks the spot where during the Hundred Years' War English troops frequently disembarked to devastate the hinterland.

Off the coast road below St Quentin is the Parc du Marquenterre, a nature reserve opened in 1973 covering some 5,500 acres along the northern edge of the Somme estuary, a haven for migratory birds. Heath, forest, marsh, dune and salting make up a remarkable area. Open from April to November, it is in three parts: dunes laid out with marked paths, lakes and marshland recently reclaimed from the sea and an observation zone equipped with "hides" for bird watchers and nature photographers. The best time to be in one of these is during periods of migration or at high tide.

Capital of the Marquenterre is historic Rue, once a thriving seaport but now five miles inland and given over mainly to horsebreeding. It may be that the town owes its name to the trade in rouge, discovered in the district and used by the warlike Belgae tribe to make their appearance more terrible in battle. Rue retains several relics of its past, among them some curious old houses in the rue des

Soufflets with little trefoil windows, a *hotel de ville* with a 15th century belfry and the site of the old port, complete with moorings, cannon and a cross of Jerusalem, from which the Crusaders set sail.

But the most impressive sight in the town is the remarkable chapel of St Esprit, a masterpiece of flamboyant Gothic and a marvel of lacework in stone, built in the 15th century to house a miraculous crucifix. Washed up on the beach at Rue in 1101, so the legend runs, the crucifix was found at Jerusalem and consigned to the waves by the Christians to prevent its violation by the Moslems. Venerated by the

The beach at Le Crotoy

townsfolk, it became an object of pilgrimage for peasant, nobleman and king alike. The chapel is overlaid with a riot of sculptural decoration, the ornate keystone vaulting being particularly striking. Like so many other religious objects in France, the crucifix was burnt during the Revolution but part was saved and now rests in a reliquary above the high altar.

Easter Monday is the time to watch the St Esprit procession in Rue, a convenient centre for this part of the coast if only it had some decent hotels and a camping site. The town is at its liveliest on market day, especially on the second and last Saturday of the month.

The ancient harbour of Le Crotoy on the northern shore of the Somme estuary suffered the agony of invasion many times in the 15th century, frequently being occupied by the English and their Burgundian allies. Nothing is left of the first fortress built in 1150 by Jean de Ponthieu and dismantled by royal decree in 1670, though there are remnants of the old fortifications and the church, otherwise modern, still keeps its fortified tower. Le Crotoy is now a fishing port and a resort claiming to possess "the only beach in the north which faces south". It is also a centre for sportsmen attracted to the wildfowling in the bay, of which you get an immense panorama from the Butte du Moulin. Known to many English people, the restaurant at the Hotel de la Baie dominated by the powerful personality of a *grande dame* named Mado is famous for its seafood which includes fish soup, grilled lobster and sole cooked in a special way and served up within an hour or two of being caught.

The Mollières or marshes on the seaward side of the panoramic highway round the bay give way to the Somme river at Noyelles, linked with Le Crotoy at weekends in season by a quaint little *chemin de fer à vapeur* or tourist train. A curious cemetery at nearby Nolette off the road to Nouvion contains the graves of nearly 1,000 Chinese employed by the British army as dockers in the 1914-18 war. The men buried there — their graves meticulously maintained like those in all British military cemeteries, their headstones inscribed with pompous phrases like "A good reputation endures for ever" and "A noble duty bravely done" — were members of the Chinese Labour Corps, recruited in North China by agreement between the two governments. Commanded by English officers, the corps numbered 96,000 at the end of the war.

The easterly drift may have given the coastline an added attraction by creating the dunes but it has also stranded many of the old seaports, the most important of which is St Valéry. From the port — in which he had been forced to wait for a fair wind — William the Bastard, the duke of Normandy born to be king, set off again in 1066

Fishing boats in the Bay of the Somme

with his invasion fleet for the conquest of England, taking "*a sword to fight with, wine to fortify him and a bishop to give him absolution.*" The event is celebrated by a tablet on the old wharf by the canal. Tradition has it that the English king Harold, captured on the coast by the count of Ponthieu, was imprisoned for a time in the bulky tower that bears his name near the end of the dyke. The picturesque old town, prettily situated on the slopes of a wooded hill, grew up round an abbey founded in 610 by a disciple of St Columban. With Le Crotoy on the far side of the bay it once guarded the entrance of the Somme against invasion from the sea. As a result it was pillaged and burned by the Vikings, occupied many times by the English during the Hundred Years' War, sacked by the Spanish troops of Charles of Austria and taken and retaken by the Catholics and Huguenots during the Wars of the League.

St Valéry still preserves its solid fortifications pierced by two massive gates, some ancient houses and the 15th century church of St Martin. Like other places along the coast, however, its one-way streets may aid traffic flow but tend to bypass the historic sights, rarely signposted. The tomb of the saint from whom the town gets its name is in a modern chapel decked with the votive offerings of the fishermen. Tucked away in a courtyard less easy to find is a more historic fishermen's shrine, the rugged little St Peter's chapel hung with models of schooners and other full-rigged ships. It was probably to this sanctuary that sailors of times gone by came to perform their vow of silence when returning from a storm-tossed voyage. On landing they would walk silently in single file to the church, hang up their votive offerings and say a prayer of thanksgiving — then, and only then, could they speak to each other or greet relatives or friends.

From the tree-shaded dyke there are fine views of the bay, across which the sunsets are deservedly famous. Navigation in the estuary is made difficult and dangerous, even at high tide, by the currents and shifting sandbanks, but the fishing — especially for shrimps and flat fish — is rewarding when the tide goes out. Bathing from the two sandy beaches *bains de la ville* on the west, *bains de la Ferté* beyond the port on the east is only feasible at high tide. At other times the sands extend literally for miles.

The most comfortable hotel in St Valéry is the Guillaume de Nor-

The Somme near St. Valéry

The beach at Mers

mandy, with views of the bay from its shady garden, but the best value is undoubtedly the little family-run Routier in the narrow Rue de la Ferte in the lower town, its restaurant between mealtimes being used as a saloon bar by the locals.

West of St Valéry is Cap Hornu, a vantage point for watching the fishing and pleasure boats following the inshore channel to and from the port. Beyond the marshes that line the southern shore of the estuary, the small fishing port of Le Hourdel occupies a miniature Finistèrre, a tongue of land that advances seawards a little more each year.

Man took the initiative in the creation of the Bas Champs, bounded on the west by Cayeux, when in the 17th century Colbert, the great reforming chief minister of Louis XIV, ordered an embankment of pebbles to be built up along the coast from Le Hourdel to Ault, closing off the once-busy harbour of Hable d'Ault to form an inland lake now given over to *chasse à la hutte* or duck shooting from "hides" at the edge of the water. At homely Cayeux a mile or more of plank walks makes it easier than it would otherwise be to cross the bank of pebbles to the extensive beach, of pebbles or sand depending upon the state of the tide. The resort is extended on the north by two unspolt annexes at the edge of permanently sandy beaches, La Molli-ère and another with the English-sounding name of Brighton. Behind the extensive dunes, shaded by pines and served by the Rue du Camp des Anglais, are villas and a restaurant or two; among the sandhills are isolated pitches for campers.

Unless you happen to have a Jeep or a Land-Rover, the only way to drive south down the coast from Cayeux is to head inland through the Bas Champs as far as Brutelles, once by the sea, then on through Hautebut, where in 1372 an English army commanded by the Duke of Lancaster disembarked to ravage the surrounding countryside. The Bas Champs end at Ault-Onival, a two-part resort with a beach of pebbles and sand built on the flanks of a dry valley suspended in the high chalk cliffs which march south for five miles to Mers. Unpretentious and typically French, Ault is one of the few resorts along this part of the coast not invaded at summer weekends by the big spenders of Paris.

The 15th-century St Pierre church, typical of many along the Picardy coast, is built of pebbles and flints mixed with stone in a checkerboard pattern. South of Ault, attractively sited in another wooded opening in the cliffs, is the peaceful garden village of Bois de Cise, with its pebble beach extended seawards by a rocky platform.

Beyond the statue of Notre Dame de la Falaise, from which the views take in a wide arc of the coast, the cliffs slope down to Mers, a modern and lively resort with fine sands at low tide and a semi-circular sweep of esplanade overlooked by the comfortable Bellevue where if the rooms are small the cooking is of a high standard. Mers is bounded on the south by the river Bresle. On the other side of the river is its twin, Le Treport, the northern gateway to Normandy. But now, on this southern frontier of our region, let us turn back and then inland from Calais, and go to Arras.

3
THE ROAD TO ARRAS

Journey along the northern border of Artois to its old capital of Arras and at times you might think yourself in Belgium. This is hardly surprising. The Fenlike landscape of the plain of Flanders sweeps on across the frontier until stopped short by the heights of Artois and many of the proudly ancient towns are Flemish as well as French, both in their style of architecture and in the names and dialect of the people. They often share a common history with their Belgian neighbours, as a result of a battle or a treaty having been first in one country and then in the other.

A canal partners the road southeast of Calais across a watery landscape as far as the Pont d'Ardres, "*the bridge beyond compare*" from which nine roads and four waterways strike out in all directions. After that, as the reclaimed marshland gives way to the hills of Artois, the scenery improves. Marking the transition is the little town of Ardres, its picturesque gabled houses grouped round a triangular Grand-Place and a church in flamboyant Gothic. Bordering the town on the north is an extensive lake popular for fishing and boating. The Hotel Grand-Clement in Ardres is well worth a visit.

In the plain between Ardres and Guines, on the west, England and France were temporarily reconciled when, in 1396 Isabella, daughter of the French king Charles VI, married Richard II at Calais. There took place, in 1520, the famous *Field of the Cloth of Gold*, when in a display of wild extravagance François I tried to forge an alliance with Henry VIII of England against the newly elected Hapsburg emperor Charles, the latest in a long line of imperialists lording it over the territory only a few miles north. But despite the pomp or perhaps because of it the meeting ended in stalemate and Artois once more became the battleground of Europe.

The English were then masters of Calais and its hinterland, and the Field was neutral ground. The boundary of the English-occupied area ran down the main street of the nearby village of Campagne, those living on the left being in one camp, those on the right the other.

East of Ardres is the ancient small town of Audruicq, with traces of its former ramparts and an 18th-century château, and on the St Omer road to the south is the village of Nordausques, from which a byway winds east to skirt the beautiful forest of Eperlecques on the left bank of the picturesque Aa valley.

The Aa joins the Neuffossé canal at the charming old town of St Omer in a setting of waterways, lakes and woods that has attracted painters for years. On the border between Artois and Flanders, the town grew up round the abbey of St Bertin, founded in 649 on an island in the Aa by the bishop of nearby Therouanne and now a melancholy ruin at the end of the main street which bears its name. Surprisingly, considering its distance from the sea, St Omer grew rich on its maritime traffic, given a boost in the 13th century by new-style boats invented by the Frisians. Some of the money went into the building of the classical mansions lining its broad regular streets and the 13-15th century basilica of Notre Dame south of the central Grand-Place: the fine Gothic nave is crowded with tombs, ex-votos and works of art.

North and east of St Omer are ancient marshlands drained by a geometric labyrinth of waterways or *watergands* encircling intensively farmed fertile islands tourable by boat. Like the people who farm the islands, growing enormous quantities of cauliflowers in summer and chicory in winter, you glide between them on punt-like craft. Set in the network of waterways are lakes, of which the Romelaere is easily the most attractive. The widest canals take the Dutch-sounding name of *becke*, not to be wondered at on this side of the town where everyone speaks a *patois* that mixes up Flemish and French. East of St Omer is the splendid forest of Clairmarais where a vast farm is all that remains of the abbey founded in 1140 by the Cistercians who, 25 years later gave sanctuary to Thomas à Becket. In the centre of the forest is the Harcelles lake, first stocked with trout by the monks, who fished it with rod and line just as local people do today.

*   *   *

On the Canal de Neuffossé at Arques, astride the Bethune road to the southeast, is the famous hydraulic lift of Fontinettes, built in

1887 and out of service now, which did the work of five locks by coping with a difference in water levels of 42ft. The canal skirts the beautifully preserved 18th century town of Aire-sur-la-Lys, which began as a fortress founded by Baudouin of Flanders in 1059 and reached the peak of its prosperity under Austro-Spanish domination in the 16th and 17th centuries. Around the wide Grand-Place are some quaint old houses, a charming renaissance guardhouse and a monumental *hotel de ville* decorated with trophies and topped by a tall belfry. The church of St Pierre shows the three different styles of Gothic architecture. One way to it is by the Rue St Pierre, lined by venerable mansions.

West of Aire, Therouanne is today little more than a sleepy village but was in turn the Gallic settlement of Taruenna, a major junction of Roman roads, and a powerful fortress town forming a French enclave in territory controlled by land-hungry Charles of Austria, who destroyed it in 1553. The equally peaceful small town of Isbergues, southeast of Aire, is famed throughout Artois for its pilgrimage church of the 15th century landmarked by a majestic tower. It was the second church built to house the tomb of the saintly Isbergues, sister of the great Charlemagne, on the spot where she died. Pilgrims flock to the church every year on May 21.

The story goes that the first Artesian wells (wells of Artois) were sunk in the 12th century at Lillers, to the south. (These are the kind in which the water rises spontaneously to the surface). One can still be seen in the courtyard of the old Dominican monastery. Nearby is the biggest and most remarkable Romanesque church in the province, with a three-storey nave and arcades in the style adopted so religiously by the Cistercians.

The ancient river port of Bethune looks inward to its Grand-Place bordered by a 14th century belfry and a new town hall. Beside the Lille road on the eastern outskirts is the chapel of St Eloi, headquarters of the all-male Confrerie des Charitables, a model of Christian virtue founded as long ago as 1188, whose members — dressed in a curious costume of redingote and cocked hat — carry the coffin on their shoulders from the church to the cemetery and comfort the bereaved.

Bethune stands at the northern edge of the great coalfield which though never more than ten miles wide runs east to the Belgian border then continues across Belgium to Aachen in Germany. In France it blackens only about 80 miles of countryside, not most of the North as so many Britons seem to think. That part of the coalfield in Artois, about 30 miles long, was opened up only in 1850. The miners work the shallow seams at depths of from 1,500 to 3,000 ft, though some go even deeper. Many industries are located on the coalfield itself, but most of the belching chimneys are over to the east. Densely populated the district may be yet there is no waste ground and the fertile soil not invaded by the paraphernalia of mining and industry is green with crops or colourful with flowers. The miners have a passion for racing pigeons. They have a great love of gardening, too.

Hallmarks of the landscape are the shale heaps rising up like miniature mountains. These were the observation posts of trench warfare in 1914-18, when the front line was now east of the Bethune-Arras road, now west of it. Yet both sides continued to mine coal to within a couple of miles of the trenches.

Some of the fiercest fighting along the 600-mile front occurred around Lens, in the plain east of the road, taken and held by the Germans for most of the war. In 1850 Lens had a population of 2,500 but by 1914 it had become the chief coal mining town of France and home to 36,000 people. It is still ringed by characteristic miners' suburbs known as *corons*, with row on monotonous row of terraced brick houses. Thousands of these are lived in by Polish immigrants and their families who came to find work in the town in the 1920's. What will happen when the coal runs out, as it is expected to do by 1985, no one knows.

Between Aix-Noulette and Arras the road becomes a pilgrimage route strung with cemeteries and memorials on ground which in 1914 was overlaid with muddy trenches, stunted trees and mounds of rubble. Buttressed by coils of barbed wire and machine guns, defences on both sides were well-nigh impregnable. Every attacking force was exposed to murderous fire that cut it down like a scythe passing through corn. The point was made with ghastly emphasis in the battle for Loos en Gohelle, a village in 1915 and now a northern suburb of Lens. It is surrounded by 14 military cemeteries in which lie some of those killed in the British attack in September-October 1915. Other results of two months of dreadful fighting? A gain of two miles on a four-mile front, three divisional commanders killed and over 20,000 men 'missing' — in other words, what was left of them could not be identified. In the jargon of the day, "normal wastage".

But the cemeteries are probably thickest where the highway climbs to the small town of Souchez, a place name that cropped up regularly in Allied communiques. East of it is the village of Givenchy and Vimy Ridge, names once equally famous. In April 1917 the British attacked on a 12-mile front running south from Givenchy, the four Canadian divisions advancing in line against Vimy Ridge bearing the brunt of the holocaust. Now a monumental memorial, completed only in 1936, and bearing the names of the 64,000 Canadians

German cemetery on the Western Front

killed in this and other battles in France dominates the ridge. Some 250 acres are Canadian property and form a park around the monument and the Grange Tunnel, still preserved as it was in 1918. West of the Bethune-Arras road, separated from Vimy Ridge by the ravine cut by the river Souchez, is the 540ft high crest of Notre-Dame de Lorette, the Verdun of the north, which in 1915 the French wrested from the Germans at an appalling cost in human life. On the crest an enormous lantern tower lit up at night soars up above an ossuary containing the remains of 16,000 unknown French soldiers, while 18,000 more who could be identified are buried in the cemetery that surrounds it.

South along the road two other places whose names have been written into history are Cabaret Rouge and La Targette, with their English, French and German cemeteries and memorials. In 1914-18 these were scenes of such unprecedented horror that if the ordinary folk of England, France and Germany had been forced to witness them they would surely have kicked out the generals and politicians and taken their soldier-children home.

Any farmer round Arras will tell you that the Kaiser's war has put down roots that go deep in the soil fertilised with human blood. Nearly 60 years after, the plough still turns up the ironmongery of destruction: shells, mines, mortars, grenades, gas canisters, rifles and bayonets. Unbelievable, perhaps, but people still earn a living collecting the scrap metal of that war, shrapnel fetching 50p, brass 100p a kilo. And those who till the soil find some 50 skeletons every year, some identifiable by their discs, some by the equipment they still grip tightly in their bony hands. Who even now can fully grasp the enormity of it all?

*　　*　　*

The war has left an indelible mark on the "heights of Artois" but surprisingly perhaps reminders of other periods still exist. On the southwestern edge of the coalfield near the old Roman road linking Bruay and Arras is the beautifully preserved and picturesque 15th century château of Olhain, moated by the river Lawe, where *son-et-lumière* performances are staged in season. South of it is Mont St Eloi, with splendid views and the ruins of an Augustinian abbey founded in the 7th century and damaged during the Revolution and the battles of 1915.

Arras, the old capital of Artois, is one of the martyred towns of France. Shattered in 1914-18 by four years of close bombardment, it has long ago been restored with sympathy and good taste. The town was famed in olden times for its cloth designed to be hung round the bare stone walls of draughty fortresses to make them more habitable and pleasing to the eye. The finely woven tapestry hangings were known as *arras* after the town that made them in such quantities. The prosperity this brought, at its height in the 17th century, is reflected in the two spacious main squares east of the long and narrow Rue Gambetta. The Grand-Place and the Petite-Place (or Place des Heros) are bordered by uniformly-styled arcaded and gabled mansions which generate a powerful atmosphere of a more stable past. The vast cellars and quarry workings beneath them were turned into an underground city in 1914 and for four years sheltered some 40,000 people while shells from German batteries screamed overhead. Above the doors of the shops in the Grand-Place you will see the heraldic signs of the local craft guilds and ruling families of former times.

Along one side of the Petite-Place is the beautiful Flemish Gothic façade of the 16th century *hotel de ville* and its 250ft high belfry visible for miles around. A hall on the ground floor has a renaissance fireplace bearing the arms of the ubiquitous Charles of Austria, whose Spanish troops ruled the town for the whole of the 16th century and the first half of the 17th. Other rooms in the building contain notable woodcarvings and furniture of the period.

The infamous Robespierre, born at Arras in 1758, was a close friend of the ill-named Lebon, mayor of the town during the Terror, who supervised the destruction of the churches and as "public accuser" fed the guillotine with victims. He would have presided at the tribunal which held court in the 16th century church of St Jean Baptiste, labelled the Temple of Reason during the Revolution.

A few steps from the *hotel de ville* is the 19th century cathedral of St Vaast, (pronounce it St Va) with an harmoniously proportioned arcade and a monumental staircase but a cold Greco-Roman interior. It replaced the church of the abbey founded in the 7th century by St Vaast, the town's first bishop, and so popular that no less than 69 other churches in the diocese are named after him. Adjoining the cathedral on the southwest is the grandiose 18th century abbey of St Vaast. Inside is a fascinating collection of valuable paintings, porcelain and, best of all, tapestries of Arras. Southwest again is the chapel of Notre Dame des Ardents, named from a fever which devastated Arras in the 12th century. The victims were cured, according to legend, by the light of a holy candle. The chapel attracts pilgrims in their thousands on May 18.

On the outskirts of Arras is the enormous citadel built by Vauban in 1674 to make sure that the Spanish troops of Charles of Austria, thrown out by the French, stayed out. But it was less effective in the Kaiser's war, earning the derisory name of La Belle Inutile.

The best restaurant in Arras and one most reasonably priced is the Chanzy, near the station, where the cuisine is of the savoury Flemish kind. Anyone who has not tasted the flamiche, the local leek and cheese quiche of the classically named owner Jean de Troy has missed a gastronomic treat. He has some fine wines and a few comfortable bedrooms as well. His wine cellars wandering deep beneath the restaurant are a good sample of the many others burrowed out of the rock beneath the town.

But let us leave Arras, and the grim reminders of the Great War, and go west again, along the Canche to a place with a name like a trumpet call, Agincourt.

*   *   *

Two of the most attractive river valleys in Picardy and Artois are, I think, the meandering Canche and its rustic tributary the Ternoise, the first flanked by marshes often mirrored in lakes, the second shrouded in poplars and elms. The Canche flows lazily through a gently sloping valley, strung at the water's edge with lush water meadows and charming old villages and higher up cloaked in dense woods. The farther upstream you go the more of a wide rural dream the country on either side becomes; even in summer I have hardly seen another car all day. For those who like to loiter the two rivers are perfect unhurried companions, though there are historic places to be found in and around their valleys, too. And for anglers there can be few better waters.

Anyone driving south on the N1, below Calais, the road the French call *la route des anglais* because so few of us deviate from it, is sure to remember the steep climb to the quaint walled town of Montreuil-sur-Mer on the abrupt north slope of a plateau forming the left bank of the Canche. The "sur mer" suffix in its name dates from the time when it stood on the river estuary, which as it silted up over the centuries has pushed back the sea for some ten miles. In those days, when the French kings controlled no more than a handful of provinces, Montreuil was the only royal port of France. No great honour, that, because it was their sole access to the sea.

Montreuil takes its name from the monastery (monasteriolum) founded there in the 7th century by St Saulve, bishop of Amiens. The former monastery church of St Saulve, part 12th century, with a magnificent nave in flamboyant Gothic and in the sacristy the finest jewelled treasure in northern France, lies east of the Grande Rue, the busy main street. So does the sumptuously decorated chapel of Hotel Dieu, of the 15th century. Appropriately enough, the Grande Rue leads south to the wide and irregular Grand-Place centred on a statue of Douglas Haig, the taciturn commander of British forces in

50

A lake in Artois

France in 1914-18, who had his "remote but central" headquarters in a château on the outskirts.

The old cobbled streets of Montreuil, like the steep Cavée St Firmin on the northern slope, are sure to remind you of Rye in Sussex. Many of the streets in this place of real charm must have resembled the Cavée St Firmin when Laurence Sterne made it the first stop on his *Sentimental Journey* through France. Like most other travellers on the Grand Tour he put up at the Hotel de France, where the Paris diligence used to call. It was there, that he engaged his amorous valet

Lafleur. "*The young fellow,*" said the landlord, "*is beloved by all the town, and there is scarce a corner of Montreuil where the want of him will not be felt; he has but one misfortune in the world,*" continued he, "*he is always in love.*"

Nowadays, the hotel with the biggest reputation in Montreuil is the Château, very comfortable, very expensive, rather formal, hidden behind a high wall and surrounded by its own gardens. But the France, with its oak beams, uneven floors and cavernous old-fashioned beds is much more my kind of hostelry and a fascinating place to stay.

On the north bank of the Canche is Neuville-sous-Montreuil with an old Carthusian monastery now used as a sanatorium. A delightful byway runs east along this side of the river. It passes through the basket-weaving village of Marles, facing Brimeux and its lake on the opposite bank. The old Roman road from Lyon to Boulogne crossed the Canche at Brimeux and when in the last century the villagers were digging peat from the marshes beside the river they discovered numerous Roman relics. Though restored a century ago, the 16th century church is one of the most beautiful in the valley.

Beyond Marenla, with its fine views of the Canche, Beaurainville was in the 11th century a powerful fortress where Harold of England, shipwrecked on the coast in 1064, was held prisoner until William of Normandy interceded for him. Ruined now, the fortress was an outpost of the narrow coastal strip forming part of the old province of Picardy hard against the western frontier of Artois.

Beaurainville stands at the head of the pretty Crequoise valley, at its most picturesque near the 18th century château of Torcy. Huddled round its quaint old church beside the Canche upstream, Aubin St Vaast is a point of departure for a detour along the Planquette, which flows south from Fressin through a bucolic landscape to empty into the marshes of the Canche. Fressin and its surroundings are featured in one of the works of the French writer Georges Bernanos, who spent his youth there attending the quaint 16th-century church and climbing the ivy-covered ruins of the feudal castle.

On its way east to Hesdin the country lane along the north bank of the marshy Canche skirts the splendid forest of Hesdin, where the locals still hunt wild boar. At the confluence of the Canche and the Ternoise, Hesdin was built and fortified by Charles of Austria in 1554. The ramparts have since been replaced by boulevards but the heart of the little town is still the vast Place des Armes bordered by houses of the period and a town hall of 1629 with a sumptuous loggia over the entrance. The Spanish troops of the Hapsburg emperor Charles held the town for part of the 16th and 17th centuries and the

52

Countryside near Fontaine

town hall was originally a palace built for the emperor's sister Mary of Hungary when she was appointed governor of the Low Countries. The old ballroom is now a theatre.

Hesdin was the birthplace of that stylish and prolific early 18th century writer Abbe Prevost, the author of the story of Manon Lescaut, shocking for its time, who was a monk for seven years before he fled to England.

In the town the Canche divides into several branches which gurgle merrily beneath little hump-backed bridges. Noted for its trout, the river is a fisherman's paradise. Members of British angling clubs who bring their membership cards with them have the widest choice of waters though restaurants and fishing tackle retailers in the riverside villages displaying the sign *location peche* sell permits for a day's or a week's fishing with little fuss.

The road beside the meandering Canche is continued east from

53

Hesdin to Monchel and Frevent by the *route des villages fleuris*. It passes through Vieil Hesdin, the site of the ancient town of that name and favourite residence of the counts of Artois until Charles of Austria razed it to the ground in 1553. Beyond is a string of flower-decked villages. After Conchy and its twin Monchel, comes Boubers, prizewinner in a recent France in Bloom contest. The riverside byway continues to the source of the Canche and the pleasant small town of Frevent dominated by its 16th century church fronted by a massive tower that combines belfry and porch. Nearby is a more recent relic of a Cistercian abbey founded in 1137 by the counts of St Pol and destroyed at the Revolution, the 18th century château of Cercampl.

Encircled by the Ternoise to the north and half hidden by the exuberant *bocage* is the small town of St Pol, the ancient capital of a powerful county to which it gave its name, peacefully invaded on Mondays when the farmers of the district bring their livestock and vegetables to market. Its ancient buildings include a convent flanked by two arms of the river and the ruined Château Neuf and Château Vieux.

An enchanting route from St Pol follows the Ternoise as it flows west in a wide loop to join the Canche at Hesdin. Set against a wooded backdrop, a score of picturesque villages line the road along the left bank of the river, nearly every one with a pretty church or a 15th or 16th century château, and sometimes a homely auberge as well. From Blangy, two-thirds of the way on, a byway leads north across the Artois plateau to Ruisseaville, on the main road linking Hesdin and St Omer, passing the hamlets of Maisoncelles and Azincourt on the left and the château and village of Tramecourt on the right.

It could well have been Tramecourt. But it was the humble village of Azincourt, which for some odd reason we call Agincourt, that gave its name to one of the bloodiest battles in English history. On Thursday 24 October 1415 the eve of the feast day of the Saints Crispin and Crispianus the tattered army of 6,000 archers and men at arms led by Henry V marched wearily north from Frevent, on the Canche, with a French force many times their number hard on their heels. They hoped to reach the safety of English-occupied Calais. But they knew they had a fight on their hands when their advance guard mounted a ridge near Blangy and sighted the French, in three great battalions like "*a host of locusts*", blocking the road to Ruisseauville.

Henry formed up his men just north of Maisoncelles and the French barely a mile away did the same, filling the space between the woods surrounding Tramecourt and Azincourt as they donned their armour and unfurled their banners. Their army contained at least 30,000 men-at-arms, who fought in armour on horseback or on foot. They had archers, too, though soldiers of this type did not count for much in the eyes of the French nobility.

The French had every reason to be confident, the English every cause to be downhearted. They were heavily outnumbered, had little or no food and were exhausted by a long march through a hostile countryside. Yet Henry had no choice between attack and unconditional surrender. Word had reached him that the French intended to ride down his archers, so he ordered each man to cut and carry a 6ft stake sharpened at both ends to stick in the ground in front, during the battle.

As the sun came up on Friday 26 October, St Crispin's Day, the English watched the French form up into three "battles", vanguard, main battle and rearguard. Henry knew his little army was more effective in defence than attack and his only hope of victory was to draw the enemy onto the arrows of his archers. So he marched his men forward until they were within bowshot. The sight of their advance roused the French, who plunged heavily forward through the mud. At the first sign of movement Henry halted his line. His archers drove their stakes into the ground and in rapid succession showered arrows on the French vanguard, piercing the joints in their armour and wounding their horses.

The mounted men at arms who survived the hail of arrows charged forward only to impale their horses on the stakes and be thrown to the ground, where the archers stabbed or clubbed them to death. The carnage was terrible. Others turned tail and fled, their armoured horses ploughing great gaps in the second French "battle" as it advanced into the English line. But the French front, so narrow that the dense masses were drawn up thirty men deep, was so tightly packed that many had no room to wield their weapons as they struggled forward. As the English men at arms felled those in front those behind were pushed forward to fall on top of them, to be suffocated or trampled to death. By this time the English archers had been driven into the woods on either side, from where they poured their arrows into the French flanks.

By this time the fighting was fierce all along the line, though it was hardest in the centre around the banner of Henry V. The king was struck several times, one blow making the great dent in the helmet that now hangs above his tomb in Westminster Abbey. After two hours of close combat the French army was in shreds, the bodies of their dead piled up around them. Shaken and demoralised, the

55

French main body put up little resistance to the English men at arms who advanced to meet them. Those who stood their ground were either killed or captured, others turned to join the rearguard, many of whom were already leaving the field.

The English stopped and looked about them, unable to believe they had won the day. They turned to their prisoners, who stood around in groups, and walked among them demanding their rank and name. While this was going on news came that an unidentified rabble was threatening their rear. A more immediate danger was a large force of French cavalry and foot soldiers forming up as if for a new frontal attack. Henry was a religious man with an ability to inspire fanatical loyalty to his men. "*If God gives us the victory,*" he had declared before the battle, "*it will be plain that we owe it to His grace.*" But his religion did not make him merciful to a conquered enemy. When battle began again the prisoners could grasp what weapons they could and set about their captors. There was only one thing to do — put to death all prisoners except those of high rank. The cruel decision was no sooner arrived at than it was put into effect, the captives having their throats cut by the archers of the bodyguard. Even more horrible, was the act of setting fire to the huts to which the French wounded had been taken, so that those inside were burned to death.

Soon the English and those captives still alive were alone on a field covered with dead and wounded. Henry sent for the heralds of both sides and asked them the name of the nearest fortress after which convention demanded the battle should be called. They told him it was Azincourt.

After burning their dead the king and his men spent the night at Maisoncelles. Next morning, loaded with booty, they made their way to Calais. With them went 2,000 high ranking prisoners, many never to return. Among them was the prince-poet Charles, Duke of Orleans and brother of the French king, who was to spend 25 long years in England before his ransom of £3,300 was paid. Behind them 10,000 Frenchmen lay dead on the battlefield. Over a hundred princes and great lords were among the fallen, their bodies stripped of anything of value during the night by the English archers and local peasants. Some were placed in a mass grave still marked by a calvary, others were taken for burial to the church of the 12th century abbey of Ste Marie au Bois at Ruisseaville — ruined at the Revolution, then incorporated in a farm which was in turn destroyed by bombing in the last war. And all that is left of the castle that gave its name to the battle are the crumbling foundations.

If the English who fought at Crécy bent the rules of chivalry, those at Agincourt ignored them altogether. The immediate result of the battle was small, but for France the long-term effects were catastrophic. Not only had a generation of French nobility been wiped out at one stroke but the shame of defeat hung for a century or more over those who followed them.

History has forgotten his name, but the story is still remembered of the scout who first brought Henry the news that the French army were barring his escape route to Calais.

"How large is their force?" demanded the king, but his scout, like most people in those days could neither read nor write, nor count above ten. The computation of such a huge army was beyond him, but he gave a plucky and accurate answer, "*I think Sire*", he said, "*That there are enough to kill, enough to capture, and enough to run away.*"

4
PONTHIEU

To say that expansive views of broad and undulating stretches of chalkland characterise the Ponthieu plateau gives little idea of the variety of its scenery. Much of the region is intensively farmed from primitive elongated villages which grew up along the highways, yet copses alternate with fields of wheat and pasture and in many places the plateau is broken by well-watered valleys, shaded by beechwoods and, in the west, covered by an extensive forest.

Though there is not much to show for it, few parts of France have had a more confused and troubled history, particularly in feudal times. Governed from the 10th century by fickle counts who paid only lip service to the French monarchy, the region was linked with the realm of the Plantagenet kings for a hundred years, when, in 1254 Edward I of England married Eleanor of Castile, countess of Ponthieu. After a brief period of freedom it was handed back to the English crown in 1360 by the Treaty of Bretigny, which cut Picardy in two. For nine years the proceeds of tithe rents and forestry were sent to England along with an annual tribute of several hundred live deer.

It was in the Ponthieu that the Hundred Years' War began at the battle of Crecy, after which English bands so ravaged the countryside that it became an abandoned waste, the villages ruined and its fields grown wild, a melancholy condition confirmed by a survey made in 1444 by the Burgundians, who then controlled the towns along the Somme forming the southern boundary of the plateau. Not until the death of Charles the Bold, Duke of Burgundy, in 1477 did the Ponthieu become an established part of the French monarchy, and even then it only gained the respite it sorely needed by contributing to the large sum of money with which Louis XI annually bought off the English king Edward IV and his marauding soldiers. "*Tribute*" said the English nobles, "*Salary*" said the French chronicler Commines, right-hand man of Louis XI. But their place was soon taken by other invaders, many of the battles between the armies of François I and Charles V being fought on the plateau while all around famine and epidemics raged.

Soldiers of every European army seem to have marched across the Ponthieu, some of them choosing to make their home there. In the 1914-18 war detachments of troops engaged in the battle of the Somme occupied rest quarters in the Nievre valley in the eastern Ponthieu. When the war ended many a demobbed British soldier married into a local Picard family and settled in the area, with the result that in the secluded villages of the district where the tourist is still something of a rarity English is fairly well understood at the café.

The Germans arrived in 1940 and ruled the region with an iron hand for four years, though they were unable to subdue the local resistance fighters who under cover of darkness guided many British aircraft in to land on the plateau.

Abbey of St. Riquier

A practical note. Traversed by four busy *routes nationales* which need to be negotiated with care, the Ponthieu is also served by a dense network of minor roads, all smooth surfaced though admittedly some are narrow. Most of the settlements on the plateau are primitive and rooms in the few hotels that do exist are simply furnished and cheap. Take the minor roads, and look ahead.

Water is not as scarce in the Ponthieu as it might at first appear, for the plateau falls away at the edge of many green valleys. From Nampont, the northern gateway to the region on the Calais-Paris highway, the river Authie meanders through marshland to the *village fleuri* of Villers, with a church containing some of the most beautiful stained glass in the north of France. A short way south another river appears, the Maye, which glides past the trim 18th century château of Arry to form a group of lakes that stretch as far as Bernay, where at the 15th century *maison de poste* facing the church the drivers of stage coaches making for Paris on the *route royale*, now the N1, stopped to change horses.

On the way to Bernay the Maye flows through the northern tip of the huge forest of Crécy, cut through by a grid pattern of 20 miles of roads, some created in the 15th century on the order of Louis XI, who frequently came to hunt the deer. Covering 10,000 acres and consisting mostly of beech and oak trees, it is a remnant of the vast forest that once extended from the Seine to the Scheldt. Dense and filled with game, it offered food and shelter to the earliest races of men, as witnessed by the Gallic sepulchres called *tombelles* and places of worship like Longue Borne, later becoming the refuge of hermits in search of silence

*   *   *

At the western edge of the forest, Forest Montiers grew up round a hermitage which later became an abbey where Charles of France, son of François I, died of the plague in his father's arms. In Roman times the village, like that of nearby Nouvion, stood at the edge of the sea, now seven miles away. Forest l'Abbaye, also at the edge of the forest, is a village of typical Picard houses. In the church, parts of which date from 1100, lies buried Jeanne de Castile, countess of Ponthieu.

Of the places on the plateau east of the forest the most important is St Riquier, the *Centule* of Roman times. In the 7th century a citizen of Centule named Riquier, converted to Christianity by two Irish monks, disciples of St Columban, retired to a hermitage in the forest of Crécy. Here in 645 he died. He was buried at Centule, where a monastery was founded in his name. By the 8th century the abbey and the town surrounding it formed one of the most formidable strongholds in Picardy, enclosed by walls inset with a hundred defensive towers. There were streets for artisans producing leather, cloth and wine, for hostelries and for the men-at-arms who guarded the town, as well as four chapels for the people and another for the nobles. Each day the citizens provided food for three hundred poor families and a hundred and fifty widows. Under abbot Angilbert, brother-in-law of Charlemagne and the "*Homer of his time*", the abbey of St Riquier was a centre of scholarship and study producing illuminated manuscripts that were incomparable works of art. The abbey continued to flourish until in 881 it was destroyed by the invading Vikings. Rebuilt, sacked and rebuilt again several times in later centuries, it never regained its former importance.

A 17th century building with traces of its 13th century predecessor, the great abbey church in flamboyant Gothic, now being restored, contains in the treasury some fine 16th century paintings, ivories, wood carvings and illuminated missals. In the abbey proper a permanent exhibition, devoted mainly to rural life in Picardy, has been set up.

The belfries that dominate many towns in Picardy are a symbol of communal liberty claimed by the citizens from their local lords, obtained in the case of St Riquier from the powerful abbot in 1128. The bell it housed called the people together in times of emergency, the building also serving as guard house and prison. At the summit of the massive belfry at St Riquier, with its four pepper-pot corner towers, was a beacon for the watch anciently kept there day and night which gave orders for the bell to be rung in case of fire or the approach of an invading army. By day either danger would be signalled by a flag pointing to that part of the town where defence was most needed.

Southwest of St Riquier on one of the highest points on the plateau is Ailly-le-Haut-Clocher, an unremarkable village which takes its name from its former high belfry, a landmark for miles around used as an observation post by the Germans in the last war until destroyed by British bombs meant for rocket launching sites further east. Inside the 13th century church, the vaulted and wood-framed nave looks like the hull of an upturned ship.

One of the few authentic remains of the Roman period in the Ponthieu crosses the plateau near Ailly. This is the *Chaussée Brunehaut*, erroneously named after the powerful 6th century Merovingian queen but in fact the great highway that ran in an undeviating line from Lyon northwest across the plateau to Boulogne, then continued on the other side of the Channel from Dover to Chester as Watling Street. This, like all others in the network built for strategic purposes, avoided all towns except those necessary for the defence of bridges on the route. Beside that part of the road through the Ponthieu, much of it still in use, many Roman relics have been turned up by the plough.

In the centuries between the Caesars and Napoleon the roads in Picardy were invariably left to look after themselves, travellers finding their way over the deep mudholes and ruts as best they could. The Roman roads were negotiable for many years before wearing out, the usual foundations consisting of oak planks covered with straw, a layer of round stones set in lead cement, another of gravel and chalk, a concrete made up of broken bricks, potsherds and other hard material and a top surface of square stones. The roads were steeply cambered to aid drainage and each autumn were dressed with oil to protect the surface from frost.

A curious feature on and near the *Chaussée Brunehaut* are the *soutterains* or underground shelters. In time of war the people living in the open country of the plateau, with no natural means of defence, needed somewhere to hide from the invader. They found it in the caverns which exist here and in other places on the chalk downlands of Picardy. Some say these were made to store water or grain but more plausible is the theory that they were originally dug for the sake of the chalk, the process of marling clay soil with lime to make it more fertile for cultivation being known since ancient times. The *soutterains* were almost certainly first occupied as hiding places in time of danger during the Carolingian period, when most of the population lived in villages and hamlets offering little or no protection. It was then, between 824 and 925, that the Vikings arrived again and again to ravage the countryside, pillaging and burning everything in their path — those who could ran for their lives, for these bloodthirsty savages from the North spared no one. The survivors might retire into these shelters — the openings are often hidden by a clump of trees — and maintain some sort of existence for years, going out in search of food only at night.

Huge subterranean retreats of this kind are found at Cramont and Hiermont to the north of the *Chaussée Brunehaut*, at Maison Rolland and Domvast to the south and at Domqueur on the road itself. Antiquaries have decided that these excavations were enlarged after the Viking invasions and were certainly occupied by the people of the Ponthieu during the many wars that followed. They may even have

Valloires Abbey

sheltered royalists during the Revolution, and were often in use as air raid shelters during the German and Allied bombardments of the last war. Most imposing are those at Domqueur, consisting of no less than fifty separate rooms cut in the chalk; the entrance to those beneath the village of Hiermont is near the church.

From Domqueur the *Chaussée Brunehaut* runs southeast to the pretty Domart valley, with its attractively-located villages of Vauchelles and Domart. Approached by avenues of shady elms, Domart lies at the foot of wooded slopes near the bubbling brook from which it takes its name. Close by the wide market place are flights of steps leading to the tall-towered 17th century church, an approach which offers tempting subjects for sketches or photographs at every turn. To the east is the valley of the Nievre, given over mainly to the processing of jute. Canaples has a pretty château, Montrelet an ancient church with a saddle-back tower pleasantly located on the hillside. Also notable are the churches of Candas and Fieffes, two rustic villages linked by roads that resemble English lanes. And no one should be put off by its dreary industrial outskirts from visiting the abbey church of Bertaucourt les Dames, a Romanesque building extensively restored but in a delightful setting which contains the ornately scupltured tomb of abbess Antoinette d'Halluin, who died in 1606. The suffix "les Dames" refers, of course, to the nuns she ruled.

Some of the most beautiful valley scenery in the Ponthieu lies along the Authie between Labroye, on the main Hesdin-Abbeville road, and Nampont. Flanked by woods and marshes, the little river follows a tortuous course to the sea, for much of the way forming the northern boundary of the Ponthieu and occasionally giving views of the wooded hills of Artois. Strung along this part of the valley, too, are some of the most charming villages in Picardy.

A few miles west of Labroye, Dompierre, ringed by woods, has a castle in which Louis XI stayed in 1464 and a 15th century church enclosed by old Picard-style houses. Opposite Ponches on the north bank of the river the imposing ruins of the ancient abbey of Dommartin, a Premontré foundation of the 12th century, are framed in a monumental gateway. The abbey church was pillaged in 1792 and its stone taken for building, though the contents were saved and some are now in the church of Tortefontaine, a short way north: effigies, tombs, statues, baptismal fonts and the oak chest which contained — they say — the surplice St Thomas à Becket was wearing when he was murdered at Canterbury. The modest village of Douriez, also on the north bank, is clustered round a vast central square where in olden times big fairs were held. Beside the river is the ruined keep of the 16th century castle and nearby is a vast collegiale church of the

A water-mill on the Authie

same period, one of the finest in the region, with some superb vaulting inside.

Douriez competes in the charm of its setting with Argoules, on the
west, its manor house, 16th century church and welcoming *auberge*
fronting on to the village green. Downstream is the ancient abbey of
Valloires and Vieux Moulin, an old water mill in sylvan surround-

ings on a lake created by the Authie. The Cistercian abbey of Valloires, founded in 1143 by the count of Ponthieu and rebuilt with a rare classical unity and elegance in the 18th century, is now a *preventorium* for children but the cloister, living quarters and chapel are open to visitors in summer. Housing the 13th century effigies of Marie of Ponthieu and Simon of Dammartin, the chapel is full of magnificent woodcarvings and separating choir and nave are elaborately-worked grilles of wrought iron.

South of the river, at the edge of the forest that takes its name, is the pleasant small town of Crécy, through which the river Maye gently flows and where an interesting 16th century church with a flamboyant Gothic porch contains some of the furniture retrieved from the ruined abbey of Dommartin. The town is at its liveliest during the annual Muguet (lily of the valley) festival on the third Sunday in May. A memorial in the main square and another on the outskirts serve to remind Anglo-Saxons how much historical importance the French attach to the battle of Crécy, which took place in the vale of Bulincamps to the east of the town — called not so long ago Crécy-la-Bataille. For the French monarchy, already weakened by powerful internal factions allied to the English, the battle was disastrous and throughout the Hundred Years' War that followed it France and England remained implacable enemies.

Warfare in feudal times was no less horrifying that it is now, though the 14th century chronicler Froissart paints a romantic picture of the campaigns of the Plantagenets, suggesting that the knight fought only for a noble cause, treating his prisoners with humanity and protecting the innocent. But the truth was that chivalry existed only for those who might be worth holding to ransom, other captives often being put to death as an incumbrance. The non-combatant suffered worse of all. Farms and villages were plundered for anything of value then put to the torch. Arson was a military operation, for, as well as foragers who pillaged the fields every army had its *boutefeux* charged with burning property and crops. On taking an enemy town, the drunken soldiery went on an orgy of looting and murder as a matter of course. Even more difficult for us to understand are those who, fresh from sacking monasteries and churches, said their prayers with an apparently clear conscience.

Some French historians maintain that chivalry even in this narrow form suffered a death blow at the battle of Crécy. The three sons of Philippe le Bel of France had died without male issue and the English king Edward III claimed the French crown as the son of Philippe's daughter Isabella. He had landed in Normandy with an army of 30,000, his aim simply being to advance north, ravaging the country-

CETTE CROIX
RAPPELLE
LA FIN HEROIQVE
DE JEAN DE LUXEMBOURG
ROI DE BOHEME
MORT POVR LA FRANCE
LE 26 AOVT 1346

JE VOVS REQVIERS TRES ESPECIALEMENT QVE VOVS ME MENIEZ SI AVANT
QVE JE PVISSE FERIR VN COVP D'EPEE (DERNIERES PAROLES DV ROI JEAN)

Where the blind King of Bohemia fell at Crécy

side as he went. But now, at the head of his men, he was being pursued by a formidable army gathered together by the newly crowned French king Philippe de Valois which included a contingent of Genoese crossbowmen.

Edward crossed the Somme into Ponthieu, making camp for the night at the eastern edge of the forest of Crécy, where he received word that the French had also crossed the river. "*We will wait for them here,*" he said. "*I am on the lawful inheritance of my lady mother.*" The small English army consisted mostly of longbowmen and men-at-arms equipped with *bombards, "which, with fire, threw little iron balls to frighten the horses*" — hardly the first cannon used in battle, as the French claim. Soon after daybreak the king said mass with his men then deployed them in three lines of battle, placing the archers in wedge-shaped salients on the flanks. The date was Saturday 26 August 1346.

That evening as his army approached the English the French king ordered the Genoese crossbowmen, who totalled about 15,000, to take up position at the front of the battle. But the Genoese, having marched twenty miles that day, were in no mood to fight and told their commanders so. A flock of ravens flew over the battlefield, followed by the crash of thunder and heavy rain, making the strings of the Genoese crossbows useless and turning the field into a sea of mud. The English longbowmen then let fly a hail of arrows so thick, says Froissart, that they fell like snow. The Genoese began to fall back, at which point the French men-at-arms cut many of them down, while the English archers continued to aim where the press was thickest. As the Genoese and men-at-arms fell, wounded or killed by the arrows and each others' blows, men and horses became hopelessly entangled. Then the French knights charged, breaking through the line of English archers. So fierce was the fighting that the earl of Warwick sent word to Edward III, lodged with his guards at a mill on the edge of the battlefield, asking him to bring up his reserves.

"*Is my son dead or hurt,*" inquired the king. "*No, sire,*" the messenger answered, "*but he is well matched and has need of your aid.*" "*Now,*" replied Edward, "*return to those who sent you and say they send to me no more so long as my son is alive. Also tell them that I command them to allow the child to win his spurs, for if God be pleased I would that this day be his and the honour thereof and to those that be about him.*" Edward's son, known to history as the Black Prince, was then sixteen years old.

By the end of the day the French were defeated. Their vast numbers, lack of discipline and the confusion created by their treatment of the Genoese all helped to bring about their downfall. As well as eleven princes, nearly 1,300 French knights and 30,000 men at arms were slain. The body of the blind Jean de Luxembourg, king of Bohemia and brother-in-law of the French king, tied to his horse during the battle so that the veteran warrior might "*strike a blow for France*", was found on the battlefield next day. His bravery is commemorated by a cross erected near the spot where he fell, beside the road that leads from Crécy to Fontaine sur Maye, and the Prince of Wales took his badge of black shield and plumes to do the old king honour and bears them to this day.

There is little else to remind one of the battle, and even the cross is weatherworn. King Edward's windmill has gone, and the plain from which the bodies of the nobles were taken for burial to the abbey of Valloires echoes in summer only to the sound of the wind rustling through yellow corn.

5
THE SOMME

Often losing itself in a green world of reed-studded lagoons shaded by poplars and willows, the Somme meanders gently westward between Peronne and Abbeville along a wide valley cut by its more powerful ancestor and lined in places by tall cliffs, in others by marshlands merging into meadows and woods. The lagoons are an invitation to embark on voyages of adventure in dinghy or punt or to angle for the big pike lurking in the shallows. Hidden in the thickets are the huts, made of logs or wickerwork and thatched with straw, ready for the duck shooter. Decoy ducks float aimlessly among the reeds or are perched, with a fine disregard for the natural habits of the birds, on poles rising high above the water. From spring to autumn this marshy country presents a riot of colour, starting with the red lichens and pink apple blossom, then the lush marsh flowers, rushes and grasses and ending with the russet-red leaves of late autumn.

Some stretches of marshland bear the black imprint of the *tourbières* from which generations of Picards have cut the peat that provided their only domestic fuel. Many of the lagoons were in fact created by the cutting of peat on a commercial scale with a *louchet*, a knife attached to the end of a long pole with which the cutter could take out blocks of the material from water several feet deep. Discoveries made when the louchet was being used, like the tusks of long-extinct animals which roamed the region in the dawn of time, no doubt prompted the archaeological research carried out in the valley in the 19th century — to which is due much of our acceptance of man's prodigious ancestry. Boucher de Perthes of Abbeville put into perspective the flint tools and other prehistoric relics found along the Somme when he declared them proof that man definitely existed half a million or more years ago.

But the recorded history of the Somme begins with the Romans'

Along the Somme

defeat of the Ambiani, the tribe inhabiting islands in the river from
which Amiens gets its name. And when their empire was threatened
by the barbarians from the north it was along the lower Somme
between Amiens and Abbeville that the Romans established their
military forts — though the moated earthworks, known locally as

71

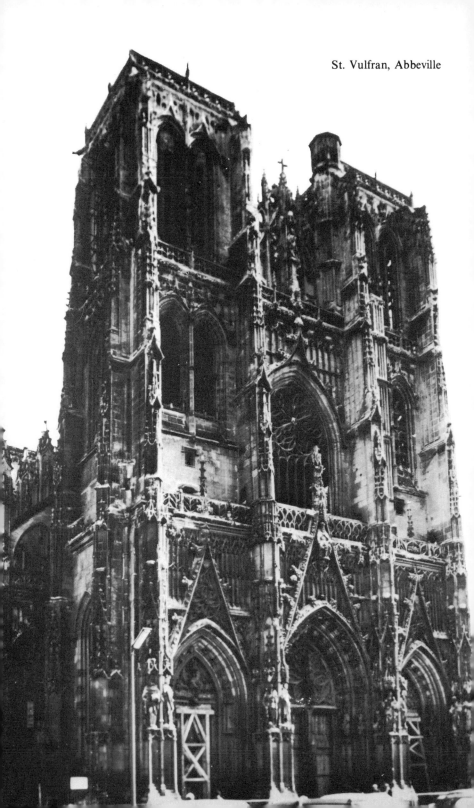

St. Vulfran, Abbeville

Camps de Cesar, and still visible at Mont de Caubert, Etoile, Chaussée Tirancourt and, most impressive of all, at Liercourt-Erondelle, were in fact built up by the ancient Gauls long before the Romans came. Just the same, the Romans must have used them as bases for their forts.

After the invasion and assimilation of the Franks many monasteries were founded, the monks clearing the forest on either side of the river to extend the cultivated area. The celebrated Benedictine abbey of Corbie, upstream from Amiens, kept the light of civilisation burning in the darkness of the Carolingian period; its writing school preserved many valuable texts and its illustrious abbot Adelard, the cousin of Charlemagne, sent his monks on evangelising missions as far afield as Germany and Denmark.

Now paralleled in places by a canal, the Somme was navigable from Corbie to the sea in medieval times. Abbeville, then a maritime port at the junction of ancient ways to Paris, London, Normandy and Flanders, owes its origin and subsequent development to the monks of St Riquier in the nearby Ponthieu. In the 9th century it was merely *Abbatis Villa*, a grange on the abbey estate, but by the 12th century the town was enjoying a remarkable prosperity, the fertile countryside flanking the river producing abundant wheat and *waide*, a plant used for dyeing which helped to create the textile industry in the valley. In 1272 Abbeville became English crown property when Edward I married Eleanor of Castile and it remained under English rule for 200 years. The town continued to thrive as a maritime port, shipping wine, wool, salt and dyes to England, though by the 18th century it was already suffering as the demand for its textiles waned and the sea receded farther and farther away.

Over the centuries the Somme, its valley sides hard to scale, its marshes difficult to cross, has many times been both a barrier and a frontier. It has seen many battles, too. Its strategic importance was demonstrated during the German invasion of June 1940, when the *Wehrmacht* postponed its drive on Paris to concentrate on Flanders and Artois, leaving only a small force on the lower Somme, along which the French army had dug in. But after the British retreat from Dunkirk the Germans brought up massive reinforcements and overwhelmed the French. But not without some cost to themselves, for some 22,000 German soldiers killed in the north of France lie buried in the cemetery above the valley at Bourdon.

In 1940 the oncoming Germans bombed Abbeville as totally as Coventry simply to terrorise the inhabitants. The hatred this engendered for the occupying *Wehrmacht* then and later was the mainspring of Picard resistance, a valuable ally later of both the Special

Operations Executive and the RAF. What had survived or been put up in the meantime was again destroyed by bombardment in 1944. Only a few of the many ancient buildings Abbeville once possessed have survived. In the town, rebuilt in the melancholy modern French style, the only structures worth a second glance are the medieval belfry, some 16th century houses, the pretty Bagatelle château and the shell of the collegiate church of St Vulfran, begun in 1488 to plans that were never completed. Its finely proportioned late Gothic façade is virtually all sculpture, that over the portals being particularly impressive. The interior is equally flamboyant. With a pleasing unity of style, the red-brick "folly" of Bagatelle was built in 1752 and contains a collection of furniture of the Louis XV and XVI periods.

Adjoining the ancient belfry a rich and absorbing collection of prehistoric finds is housed in the Boucher de Perthes museum, named after the archeologist who in the last century became one of the founders of the science of prehistory.

The lower Somme between Abbeville and Amiens is probably the more historic, the upper reaches between Amiens and Peronne the more scenic, though there are plenty of exceptions. History and scenery combine at Longpré les Corps Saints, a straggling village hidden in luxuriant foliage where in the 14th century the church was burned by the soldiers of the English king Edward III. The suffix "les Corps Saints" refers to the reliquary treasures sent back from Constantinople by the Crusader knight Alleaume de Fontaine, who founded the church in 1190 and whose effigy dwarfs the crypt. Joining the Somme at Longpré, a fine fishing and boating centre, is the little Airaines stream where many a wildfowler hastens the end of many a wild duck.

Long, on the opposite bank of the Somme, is one of the most delightful of villages. Perched on high ground around its church and 17th century château, it overlooks lakes and marshes ringed by woods and thickets and strewn with water lilies and reeds. In the 19th century, when Long lived on its trade in peat, Corot and the English artist David Murray found subjects galore for their paintings beside the large stretches of water extending for several miles along either side of the valley. Coquerel, also high above the river, has a quaint little church dedicated to John the Hospitaler with an exquisite spire of openwork stone tracery which set the trend for other places of worship along the Somme, where the Gothic style continued long after it had been superseded elsewhere.

The church at Fontaine, an architectural gem of late pointed work, is full of intriguing detail, particularly the porch topped by a statue of St Aubin. Upstream, the flamboyant church of Hangest, a

74

Bagatelle Chateau, Abbeville

village renowned for its *cressonnieres* or watercress beds, contains furniture from the nearby Abbey du Gard, the 18th century buildings of which are now being restored.

In a picturesque setting to the east is Picquiny, a point of defence when the lower Somme formed the frontier between territories controlled by the Burgundians and Louis XI. The size of its ruined castle above the river, which encloses a 13th century church, vaulted kitchens, underground halls and dungeons, shows how important a place it was. A temporary bridge erected across the river near the castle in 1475 was the scene of a meeting between Louis XI and Edward IV of England. Mistrustful of each other, the two kings surrounded by their guards shook hands through a palisade set up in the centre of the bridge. The wily Louis XI persuaded Edward IV, intent on invading Picardy, to sign a seven-year truce, paying him in return 75,000 goldcrowns to take his army home and an annual subsidy of 50,000 crowns thereafter. As they used to say, the English win the battles

75

but the French win the treaties. Having bought off the English in this way, Louis XI was able to defend Picardy more effectively against the Burgundians. He also hoped for revenge, historians claim, for the humiliating treaty Charles the Bold had forced him to sign after capturing him at Peronne seven years earlier.

Textiles are still produced at Amiens, the venerable capital of Picardy astride the Somme, its velvet being world-famous since the 18th century. It was the prosperity gained from the town's trade in cloth which made it possible for the citizens to win their municipal liberties from their feudal lords, though only after a bitter fight and many calls to the king. The same prosperity, at its peak in the 13th century, also provided the funds for the building of the gigantic cathedral, the biggest in France, a focus of hope for a suffering people decimated by war and plague. It was designed by Robert de Luzarches

Rooftops and Cathedral of Amiens

and built in under 50 years between 1220 to 1269. The interior, with its vaulted nave supported by over a hundred slender pillars soaring to a giddy height, is a veritable museum of 16th century craftmanship, the choir stalls displaying some of the most beautiful wood carvings in the world. Among the innumerable sculptures some above the stalls in the south aisle depict the Spaniard St Firmin, the martyred first bishop of Amiens, against a background of the 15th century city complete with cathedral, belfry and ramparts. The famous sculpture above the porches on the west front which inspired John Ruskin to write the Bible of Amiens, translated into French by Marcel Proust, represents the Virgin on the right, Christ in the centre and St Firmin on the left; on the gallery above are statues of the French kings.

An elegant and animated centre best viewed from the top of the

Coming to market, Amiens

340 ft high Perret tower near the station (which also gives an astonishing sight of the cathedral), Amiens has some splendid public buildings and miles of leafy boulevards. But not all is new. North of the cathedral is the old St Leu quarter, intersected by streams and canals, branches of the Somme or its tributaries. A central feature is the main canal adjoining the Place Parmentier, where on weekdays the Marché sur l'Eau is held. Vegetables sold in the market are carried there on long flat-bottomed boats, a cross between a gondola and a Thames punt navigated with a single oar. They come from the nearby *hortillonages*, market gardens with their rich black soil sur-

rounded by water and accessible only by boat, typical of the marsh cultivation practised for generations along the Somme. Boats making a tour of the islands leave from the café on the Ile aux Fagots and from the Pré Porus.

The elongated central area south of the cathedral extends from the station to the modern Maison de la Culture, an arts centre open to all where exhibitions and similar events are always being put on. The Promenade de la Hotoie on the northwest is all that a town park should be and no one should grudge an hour or two to the Picardy museum, a splendid building containing exhibits covering the art of the province through the ages, notably the 17th and 19th century schools of paintings as illustrated by the work of local artists. One room is given over to the work of the Confrérie du Puy Notre Dame d'Amiens, a medieval guild of painters, the master of which was required to contribute each year a canvas glorifying the Virgin which until 1723 was offered at an altar kept for that purpose in the cathedral. About a dozen of them, dating from 1499 to 1523, have survived. Anyone avid for more should make for the Hotel de Berny, built in 1634 to house the tribunal of treasurers of France in the Government of Picardy and now turned into a museum of local art and regional history.

In Celtic times Amiens bore the name Samarobriva, the "bridge on the Somme" which when the Romans conquered Gaul carried one of their most important highways across the river. The Frankish kings Childeric and Clovis made the city their capital, and later the Normans fortified it. The Treaty of Arras assigned Amiens to the dukes of Burgundy, but Louis XI bought it back in 1463 only to lose it again a few years later. Amiens was finally joined to the French crown in 1470, though it remained in the forefront of battle as a *ville frontière* until the annexation of Artois in 1659.

Amiens is a convenient centre for excursions to four interesting sights in the Amienois, once a feudal fief controlled by the lords of the city which extended north and south into the Picard plain. In the south, the church at Sains en Amienois is notable for its sculptured panel of the 13th century which portrays the martyrdom of the saints Fuscien, Victorix and Gentien, beheaded at the side of the Roman road from Amiens to Breteuil one winter's evening in 375. Just short of Breteuil on the left bank of the Noye near the source of the river is Folleville, seat of the powerful Lannoy family, whose head, Raoul, was counsellor to three kings: Louis XI, Charles VIII and Louis XII. High on the hill is the tower of the once great castle and nearby is the delightful small church, with a carved roof and benches of the 14th century and the magnificent altar tombs of the Lannoys.

North of Amiens is the pretty 18th century château of Bertangles, approached by a majestic avenue of lime trees. Beyond it is Naours, famous for its underground shelters (*muches* in Picard dialect) discovered by the curé of the village in the late 19th century. Four entrances lead to thirty galleries or streets off which are over 50 rooms, with wells to the water beneath and outlets to the air 100ft above. Some dates carved on the walls go back to the Hundred Years' War. The caves were used by the British army in the Kaiser's war and in 1943 became an important German munitions base. It would need a census to prove it, but the villagers of Naours are supposedly noted for their big feet (*les grands pieds de Naours*).

As it makes its serpentine way west to Amiens the upper Somme, enclosed by exuberant fauna, has a secretive pastoral character. For much of its winding course the river is lined by lakes, most extensive near the big village of Clery. The valley is lined by poplars but the villages along it shelter beneath tall elms. The Somme provides superb fishing for eel, pike, carp, perch and bream and at many places along the river what looks like a camping site may well turn out to be private land divided into plots leased by local anglers, on which they put a chalet or a caravan. There are proper camping sites, of course, but like hotels they are few and far between.

Bray, once a river port and now a popular angling centre, is folded in a wide loop of the Somme, its cobbled streets dominated by the massive tower of its church, in part romanesque. From the cliffs above the river, notably at Curlu and the Belvedere de Vaux, there are extensive views, as there are at La Neuville sous Corbie where the wonderfully detailed and original sculptured portal of the 16th century church pictures Christ entering Jerusalem. The church is one of the few ancient buildings to have survived in this area, bitterly fought over under impossible conditions in 1918 and in places still pockmarked by shell holes.

Nearby Corbie, set between the branching valleys of the Somme and the Ancre, is a lively small town centred on a twin-towered Renaissance *hotel de ville*. Of the great Benedictine abbey of 500 monks founded in 657 by Bathilde, wife of Clovis II, little more than two churches remain, though some of the abbey treasures have been preserved. The church of St Etienne has a fine 12th century façade that of St Pierre, its portal flanked by tall towers, was the nave of the old abbey church and contains the imposing 15th century tomb of Raoul de Roye. At the junction of the roads to Albert and Bray stands the statue of Ste Coletee, the visionary daughter of a 15th century carpenter of Corbie and the object of a yearly pilgrimage for many Picards.

Valley of the Somme

On the main Amiens-Peronne road a short way south of Corbie is Villers Bretonneux, a straggling unattractive village with a famous name. The road, an old Roman highway, was closed in spring 1918 by the last-ditch stand of the Australian Corps. The 10,000 who died there are commemorated by a huge monument on high ground to the northeast from which there are panoramic views of the valley of the Somme and of Amiens cathedral.

The historic fortified town of Péronne, where the castle in which Louis XI was imprisoned still stands, is surrounded by lakes created by the Somme. Islanded in the lakes are the *hardines*, fertile market gardens similar to the *hortillonnages* of Amiens. Eels taken from the lakes are either smoked or made into a paté to provide two local deli-cacies. Most leisure activities at Péronne, too, are concerned in one way or another with water. The town has often been attacked and besieged, most memorably by the Spanish troops of Charles of Aus-tria in 1536, when the courageous Marie Fouré galvanised the towns-folk into fighting back. In 1870 Péronne was bombarded by the Prussians and during the 1914-18 war was reduced to a shapeless ruin by shellfire while occupied by the Germans. At the edge of the wide main square is the charming renaissance *hôtel de ville*, flanked by two towers. So long as it is not approaching his sacred two-hour lunch period the *concierge* will open up the Musée Danicourt of Gal-lic coins and relics found in Merovingian tombs in the district. Pér-onne may not be Nice but it has its Promenade des Anglais, too, though in this case it commemorates stout-hearted soldiers rather than sun-seeking milords.

From Péronne upstream the Somme is less attractive, about the only place of note along it being the village with the monosyllabic name of Y off the road to Ham. They do say there are families in the district with single-letter surnames, too. But let us leave Amiens and go east, to Albert.

*   *   *

Apart from impeccably-maintained cemeteries, the irregular land-scape northeast of Albert, bisected by the Ancre valley and dotted with small villages and hamlets, displays at first sight few reminders of the holocaust that took place there some sixty years ago. The Bat-tle of the Somme began in late June 1916 when the 1,600 guns behind the British front line fanning out either side of the road to Bapaume bombarded the German defences night and day for a week, sending man-size shells hurtling through the air with the noise of an express train to deafen the soldiers of Kitchener's volunteer army keeping watch from their trenches over a desolate no-man's-land of barbed wire entanglements and mine craters, and then explode in the Ger-man lines. The bombardment was the prelude to the greatest com-bined British and French offensive of the war, timed to begin early on the morning of July 1.

In preparation for the Battle of the Somme, as the offensive was called, British and Commonwealth troops in France had by June 1916 risen to a million. Haig, the British C-in-C, had insisted on this number before committing himself to the battle, for he held firm to his belief that a mass attack was the only way to break through the

Hôtel de Ville, Péronne

German defences. He also shunned new methods such as night operations and was not impressed by novelties like the tank. Quietly confident, reserved and self disciplined, Haig was an administrator who looked only at what he wanted to see and listened only to what he wanted to hear. His declared policy was to "*go on hitting the Boche and make him retaliate till he's spent*", a policy which, as he interpreted it, was to decimate his own army much more than that of the Germans.

In 1916 the Tommies still respected their officers, though much of this respect had been heroically earned by the subalterns and lieutenants at the Front enduring much the same conditions as their men. British soldiers in the Somme trenches, many of whom sported the handlebar moustaches then fashionable at home, were given a cold meal and tea twice a day, the meal usually consisting of biscuits and *boeuf bouilli* or, as they pronounced it, bully beef. These were the "New Armies" and though few of them had been in battle before,

Monument to the missing Theipval

morale was high, for it seemed certain that they would break through the German lines long before the winter set in. With half as many again in reserve, eight British divisions commanded by Rawlinson were joined on their right flank by French forces totalling five divisions. The two armies faced only six German divisions commanded by von Stein and von Pannwitz which formed part of von Below's Second Army, with its headquarters at St Quentin to the southeast.

Yet this was not the best part of the Allied line from which to launch an offensive, most of the British troops occupying low-lying positions which put them at a distinct disadvantage. Established mainly on high ground, the Germans had built extensive fortifications with up to four lines of defence. The front embraced many ruined villages, the Germans using the cellars at the front of the houses as firing positions and those at the back as bomb-proof shelters.

Tunnelling into the limestone subsoil of the Somme is not difficult and the German sappers had burrowed 30 feet down to create underground shelters furnished with tables, chairs and sometimes even a piano. More extensive diggings were fitted out with kitchen ranges,

Mine crater on the Somme, at La Boisselle

electric light, telephones, lavatories and rest rooms. (These seemed safe until their entrances were blown in by shellfire, burying their occupants alive). The German machine gunners were trained to remain below during a bombardment, returning to the surface with their weapons intact when the shelling stopped.

The British infantryman's greatest fear was the barbed wire, up to 40 yards deep in front of the enemy positions, for he knew that if caught on it he would be a sitting target. The main purpose of the week-long bombardment was to cut openings in the wire to allow the infantry through, but because the British gunners had only a limited number of explosive shells it did so in only a few places. Yet the attack went ahead as planned. Ten minutes before zero hour on July 1st 1916 several huge mines placed by the British beneath the German forward positions were blown, raining down debris for fully half a minute and forming huge craters, killing many Germans, but of no real assistance to the advancing British troops.

At 0730 the British infantrymen, each carrying 60lb of equipment, emerged to advance across the open in straight lines. North of the Albert-Bapaume road the attack failed miserably, German machine gun and rifle fire stopping most of the British soldiers near their own wire, the remainder getting only as far as the first German trenches. South of the road the attack had more success, on the French front most of all. Yet the British casualties on the first day alone totalled 57,470, nearly half the number of men engaged.

Like a huge machine, out of control, the offensive rolled on for four and a half months, producing the heaviest losses in British history for a gain of 45 square miles of enemy-held territory. Then in March 1917 the Germans made a strategic retreat to the Hindenburg Line they had secretly established to cover Douai, Cambrai and St Quentin, devaluing the heroic efforts put in earlier to dislodge them. The Battle of the Somme killed or wounded over a million men, a figure difficult to comprehend, and impossible to justify.

*   *   *

In the Place d'Armes at Albert is the neo-Byzantine basilica of Notre Dame des Brebières housing the venerated 12th century statue of the Vierge aux Brebis, an object of pilgrimage still. The golden Virgin atop the church tower, visible for miles around, replaces the damaged original which from 1916 to 1918 hung face down over the town. The troops believed that when the Virgin fell the war would end, and after she fell it did. Inside the Flemish-style *hôtel de ville*

86

fronting on the spacious main square, the town's coat of arms is decorated with the *croix de guerre* and the *legion d'honneur*, for Albert was in the midst of the fighting for 29 months of the war. Old soldiers would find it difficult to recognise the little town now, so prosperous and animated has it become.

Two miles northeast along the road to Bapaume is the former German held village fortress of La Boisselle, where a huge crater from a British mine near the head of "Sausage Valley" is 60 feet deep and 240 feet wide. The Northumberland Fusiliers in attacking La Boisselle on the first day of the offensive lost 6,000 men but by July 15

British cemetery at Rancourt

had pushed the front forward of the village. South of the Bapaume road the landscape is open, which may explain why the British had more success on this side, evidence of which is the German cemetery at Fricourt, a fortified village in the angle of the German line. Beyond nearby Mametz is High Wood (Bois des Fourneaux), the scene of bitter fighting from July to September.

One of the few places where the German wire had been cut on July 1 was in front of Montauban, the bombardment also preventing any food reaching the defenders. As a result the Manchesters and Scots Fusiliers captured and held the village, over a mile inside the German lines. The road leading from Montauban to Guillemont, in 1916 *"straight, desolate and swept by fire"*, is continued by another to Ginchy. The byway from Ginchy to Longueval passes Delville Wood: of the 3,150 South African troops who attacked the German positions there on July 1 only 750 had survived five days later. The South Africans finally consolidated their position on July 17 and had to withstand repeated German attempts to drive them off. In the now-silent wood a monument to the men who died casts its shadow on a British and South African cemetery in which many of them are buried.

From Longueval the road through bleak open country to Maricourt passes Bernafay Wood and Longueval Road cemetery, in which lies one solitary German who fell like most of the British on either side of him in October 1916. On the way to Bapaume, the unremarkable village of Flers was captured as late as September 15 in the first attack with tanks. Churchill later criticised Haig for using the new weapons in indecisive operations, saying they should have been massed in one sector where they might have achieved an important breakthrough. Combles, where the Germans occupied a system of fortified and interlinked cellars and quarries known as the Maze, has a British military cemetery adjoining the communal one. East of the Autoroute du Nord, which marks the limit of the British right flank, is a church at Rancourt dedicated to the French who died in the battles of Picardy; behind it is a cemetery in which French soldiers are buried, most of whom were killed in the autumn of 1916. Beside the road from Rancourt to Combles is a sombre German cemetery, with black wooden crosses marking the graves of men also killed in the autumn of 1916. Cemeteries, Cemeteries, Cemeteries, the graveyard of a generation.

In the region north of the Albert-Bapaume highway there are wide views from the ridge-tops and none at all in the vales at the base of the folds. Along one of these flows the pretty Ancre stream, enclosed by willows and tall poplars; on a spur above the river near Albert is

French cemetery at Rancourt

Aveluy Wood, in the heat of July 1916 fought over yard by yard. Off
the road to Authuille, on the left bank of the Ancre, a footpath leads
to Blighty Valley, less a valley than a tranquil corner disturbed only
by birdsong. Most of the soldiers buried there, some no more than 18
years old, died in the first day's fighting. Pozières, on a ridge beside
the Bapaume road, was captured by the Australians in July; in the

Trenches and memorial to the Newfoundland Regiment, Auchonvillers

cemetery is a monument to some 14,000 men who disappeared during the Battle of the Somme.

Occupying a broad east-west platform, Thiepval was the most heavily defended village in the German line. For three months its name appeared constantly on communiques. It is still prominent, for its gigantic British memorial bearing the names of 73,000 men with no known grave dominates the skyline. The 18th division of Kitchener Volunteers from the Home Counties and East Anglia was one of only four divisions which had any success on July 1. Attacking on a front a mile wide it captured Trônes Wood by the middle of the month and by mid-September Thiepval itself. On July 1 the 36th Ulster Division captured and held a fortified fieldwork half a mile northwest of Thiepval known as Schwaben Redoubt, all traces of which have long since disappeared. But the Tour de Belfast monument beside the road to Hamel remains to commemorate the Ulstermen's courage.

Beaumont Hamel lies amid the ravines of the Ancre. On July 1 the British 29th division attacked the German-held village, losing nearly 5,000 officers and men killed or wounded, and it was not until November 19 that it was eventually captured. At Auchonvillers thirteen men of the Border Regiment are buried in the communal cemetery, at the edge of the village as most French cemeteries are. In spring the white blossom of hawthorn appears on Hawthorn Ridge, beyond which is the memorial park embracing ground over which the Newfoundlanders fought on the first day of the battle. The trenches and shell holes have been preserved, their edges softened by carefully trimmed grass. Sheep graze on the fringe of the park, centred on its caribou monument and ringed by several cemeteries. Below the caribou, the symbol of Newfoundland, an orientation table gives clues to the battleground where in 1916 what had been 25 villages and eight woods was little more than a lunar landscape. Most of the male population of Newfoundland died in twenty minutes under the machine guns of the 'Y' ravine. Yet amid all this destruction one building which did survive was the 16th century Gothic church of Mailly-Maillet, west of Auchonvillers. Built under the patronage of Isabeau d'Ailly, wife of Jean III de Mailly, its spendid flamboyant portal depicts biblical scenes, a fine example of Picard religious sculpture.

Although the battlefield covered a relatively small area (the British front extended some eight miles either side of the Albert-Bapaume road) it is only possible in one day to see the more important monuments. Access to some cemeteries is rough and feasible only on foot along unmetalled tracks as muddy in wet weather now as they were in 1916. A register of graves is kept at every cemetery.

Some meadows in the area still show the scars of craters and ploughing still turns up the occasional shell. Over the years the plough and the harrow have smoothed the contours of the land like a giant hand and the resilient earth, shaded now by mature trees, produces rich crops and lush pasture. But in the cornfields the bright red

91

splash of poppies still appears in summer and the rebuilt villages keep a 1914 look and an enclosed atmosphere that shuts out the stranger, making them seem just as foreign to present-day Anglo-Saxons as they must have done to the soldiers of Kitchener's Army.

It's a tragic place, but you should go there. This is the place where Britain and its Empire bled to death.

*   *   *

But enough of death and bloodshed, let us go to the Vimeu.

In the heat of summer as in the mists of autumn, the rural charm of the Vimeu, undisturbed by a single town of any size, is the perfect antidote to urban claustrophobia and kahki ghosts. An undulating limestone plateau bordered on one side by the Somme and on the other by the river Bresle which marks the border of Normandy, it is overlaid with a dense network of byways from which the views are at one point extensive, at the next enclosed. The wooded landscape, with its empty roads and its rustic villages set among lush meadows and fields of wheat and often hidden by orchards and tall trees, reflects the English countryside as it must have looked at the turn of the century. Here the unpolluted rivers are rich in trout, the air is breezy and pure and the everyday sounds are those of the farmyard: the lowing of cattle, the clucking of fowls and the barking of a dog guarding sheep.

In this often-embattled region there is little of the spectacular. The sights are more often on a more homely scale — pretty villages, scenic valleys, quaint churches, old windmills and the like — but to the traveller with an enquiring mind they are no less interesting for that. Many of the villages have names ending in *court*, indicating that they developed from a *corcis* or group of fortified farms occupying a knoll or bluff and shaded by leafy elms.

The history of the Vimeu is mainly one of foreign invasion, by the ferocious Vikings, then the English and the Burgundians during the Hundred Years' War, followed by the Spanish troops of Charles of Austria who crossed the border frcm the Low Countries. Why the Vimeu is so lacking in monuments to the past is partly explained by the destruction these invaders caused, but another reason is the local limestone which, while it is easy to work, is too soft to withstand the effects of the weather for long.

The Kaiser's war may not have touched the Vimeu but the Germans arrived in strength in 1940, remaining in occupation until 1944 and causing hardship and suffering impossible to imagine by anyone

The Church at Mailly-Maillet, on the Somme

who did not experience it. Inland, most of the soldiers of the Wehrmacht lived in casemates outside the villages and unlike the hand-picked troops guarding Hitler's Atlantic Wall along the coast were old men whose only means of transport was a bicycle. For several years during the War the course of the Somme marked a division between the Vimeu and the territory north of the river, a forbidden zone administered from Brussels, though the demarcation line was not difficult to cross. Resistance was active in the region, a clandestine newspaper *La Picardie Libre* being regularly published and RAF Lancasters dropping arms and explosives that the *maquis* used to blow up railway lines and stations and anything else that might be of use to the Germans. Many courageous local people secretly operating under the emblem of the *hirondelle* or swallow who were deported or shot by the Germans are still remembered.

The Picards of the Vimeu also mourn some of the villages sacked by the English during the Hundred Years' War. At the edge of a great forest on the south, Arguel is dominated by an escarpment from which a castle once looked down on the village, then large and with a population of 1,800. In 1402 the English stormed the castle and sacked the village, only 22 of the inhabitants escaping with their

Château at Rambures

lives. The site of the castle is now marked by a calvary around which the people of Arguel, now numbering less than sixty, each year commemorate the sad episode by holding an open-air mass.

Arguel stands in the pretty Liger valley, a tributary of the Bresle. Several places beside the smaller river are centres of a cottage industry devoted to chair making which grew up because the necessary woods — oak, ash and beech — are close to hand. They include Hornoy, with its brick-built château, and St Aubin Riviere, with one of the few wood frame and plaster churches in France.

North of Arguel, close by the almost-English scene of a village green where geese feed beneath trees that cast their shadow on a little church, stands the 15th century moated fortress of Rambures, one of the most complete feudal strongholds in existence. Built to resist the English during the Hundred Years' War, it formed a French enclave in an area dominated by the invader and earned itself the title of the "*Key to the Vimeu*," in the space of two centuries being taken, burnt, retaken, destroyed and rebuilt again and again. The castle's redbrick keep and bow-fronted façade is flanked by four enormous round towers, grim and near-windowless, with turrets above the machicolations, the whole culminating in a medley of dormers and pointed roofs. The overhanging upper storey of two of the towers is cut away to form a recessed balcony where important prisoners were exhibited in iron cages. The lower part consists of three storeys of dungeons, some of them below the level of the moat and entered only by *oubliettes*.

Inside the castle, which has remained in the same family since the 15th century, the rooms are decorated with valuable period furniture, portraits of the Rambures family over the centuries, tapestries and *objects d'art*. Like many another Picard squire, David, lord of Rambures, was killed at the battle of Agincourt in 1415.

Châteaux and manor houses exist elsewhere in the region but more interesting perhaps are the parish churches, well cared for and often more imposing than seems justified by the size of the communities they serve. Some of the most beautiful are those in and around the pretty village of Moyenneville (Middletown to us), with sculptured friezes and wood-framed ceilings above a nave shaped like the upturned hull of a ship.

The flamboyant Gothic church at Toeufles, of the 13th century, has some interesting choir stalls and other ancient furniture. That at Acheux, built around the same time, has an Anglo-Norman choir: in the same village is Autheux chapel, a place of pilgrimage to St Fiacre, patron saint of gardeners. There are other churches in this style at Behen and Tours en Vimeu. Acheux is close by the Autheux or

Zoteux valley, lined with copses as far as Acheux Wood, from where there are fine views.

Surprising in the boldness of its conception, the church at Mian-nay, also with a wood-framed ceiling above the nave, has a belfry nearly 90ft high. From the church of Maisnieres, with its roma-nesque nave built in 1100, the wooded Vimeuse, noted for its trout, flows into the Bresle at Gamaches, where the bigger river forms a wide stretch of water popular with anglers and dinghy sailors. Cen-tred on its enormous market place, Gamaches was once noted for glass making, founded on the order of Louis XIV but now in decline. The restored 12th century church of St Pierre and St Paul had some elegant arcades. Not far away are the *cahutes*, curious caverns that were lived in until 1939. The lively fair of Gamaches, held on the first Wednesday in May and October, is one of the oldest in France.

Another pretty valley in the Vimeu is the Liger between Liomer and Senarpont, where the St Claude tree, decorated with *ex-votos* and strips of cloth, forms an unusual object of pilgrimage. Around Liomer, an attractive village, are some typical Picard farms.

The Picard farm combines home, stables and granary on a plan designed to keep out the intruder. Windowless walls of storage build-ings flank the big doors that seal the entrance to an inner courtyard, giving most village streets a rather sullen air. The inner courtyard is where the farmer usually lets his *basse-cour* — chickens, ducks and geese — range free. On the far side of this is the farmhouse proper, the flanks being closed off by stables and granaries. Many farms now have walls of brick but there are still some built in the traditional way with a timber frame covered with *torchis*: lath or wattle daubed over with a mixture of clay, lime and straw, which soon cracks but is easy to renew. Behind the farmhouse is the *potager* or kitchen garden.

The oldest church in the Vimeu, and the most interesting, is in the ancient small town of Airaines, developed from a Roman station and over the centuries invaded twenty times. At the side of a hill and almost all gable and roof is the transitional romanesque church of Notre Dame, built in 1130. Below the primitive ogival vaulting is a baptismal font of the 11th century, designed for total immersion, and the 13th century tombstones of Henri, sire of Airaines, and his wife Catherine. Someone living nearby will give you the key if the church happens to be locked.

Other sights in the town are the ruins of the 13th century castle of the Duc de Luynes, in which the English king Edward III is supposed to have slept when on his way north to Crécy with his army in 1346, Roman entrenchments and the 16th century flamboyant Gothic church of St Denis. The marshy valley of Airaines on the northeast is

Church at Airaines

A gîte in the Vimeu

less for admirers of pastoral scenery than for anglers and wildfowlers who set out from Bettencourt, a village with its church curiously placed among the houses on the hill.

On the outskirts of Huppy, noted for its top-quality cider, is a church in flamboyant Gothic with stained glass dating from 1545 and a chapel for the local lord with a fireplace by which he could keep warm while praying in winter. The view taking in the church and the nearby château is pleasant. The château, built of stone and brick, incorporates a tower that served as a prison and in the park surrounding it is an avenue of mature trees. One is an elm nearly 20ft round, used not so long ago as a "tree of justice" by the local seigneur, in other words, for hanging the wrongdoers.

Allery has a 16th century church with a massive belfry and the pretty village of Hallencourt another with carved framework bearing Gothic inscriptions dated 1493. Up to the turn of the century the Vimeu — the granary of Picardy — ground its corn close to where it grew, and wind and water mills were common. South of Huppy is St Maxent with the sole surviving windmill in the region.

While it has no belching chimneys nor the sordid surroundings that usually go with them the Vimeu does have its industry. Developed from crafts practised by the peasants at home in winter, it consists of small factories in the valleys around Fressenneville and Friville-Escarbotin processing textiles and metal. A lot of the metal is fashioned into locks and taps, an activity which began they say when Flemish clockmakers followed the Spaniards from the Low Countries who occupied the Vimeu in the early 17th century. But the main industry in the region is still farming, though with the three-generation family now rare many of the farmers employ immigrants to do the work their absent sons and daughters would formerly have done.

"*No scattered farmhouses in this part of Picardy, all being collected in villages, which is as unfortunate for the beauty of the country as it is inconvenient to its cultivation,*" wrote Arthur Young. He might have been less critical had he known that centuries of invasion and brigandage made it necessary for the peasants of this vulnerable region to live close together for mutual protection, a tradition that lingers on.

The fields the farmer cultivates or devotes to grazing usually lie outside the village. There are no hedges to divide one man's land from another's though the boundary is often marked along the roadside by a calvary. A common sight outside the villages in late afternoons in summer is the peasant milking his cows in the fields where they graze. Many of the meadows are shaded by tall elms beneath

99

which the cattle can shelter, but then, there are mature trees surrounding nearly every village in the Vimeu. On the rare occasions that local people travel outside the district it is their well-wooded environment they miss the most.

In an area as rural as the Vimeu luxury hotels are as thin on the ground as sophisticated night spots. There are a few hostelries, of the kind the struggling French bagman might use, but better to stay on a farm, in a *gite* or furnished cottage or your own tent or caravan. May you be as fortunate as I was when I stayed in the *gite* on the de Colnet family's farm at Quesnoy-Le Montant. With typical Picard directness, de Colnet insisted that I shared the excellent food and the dangerously-drinkable home-made cider at his table while he entertained me with his wide knowledge of the history of the region.

6
BEAUVAIS AND THE PICARDY PLAIN

Visible for miles across the *plaine picarde*, the cathedral of Beauvais was one of the few ancient buildings left standing in the town after German bombs had rained down on it in early June 1940. Yet if no other reminders of the town's historic past had survived, the Gothic church of St Pierre would in itself more than justify a visit. For this, though never finished, is both the tallest and the most beautiful cathedral in all Christendom.

At the foot of the immense choir, 204 feet high, is part of the humble Basse Oeuvre, the first primitive cathedral built during the reign of the Carolingians. The second, the Nouvelle Oeuvre, begun in the 10th century, was burned down in 1180 and again in 1225. The bishop and chapter then decided to rebuild it on a much greater scale, devoting one-tenth of their considerable revenues to the project.

From the beginning it was an unfortunate sequence of daring planning, construction and collapse. The abside and choir were begun in 1272. They fell down in 1284 and it took nearly half a century to clear the ruins. At the end of the 14th century only the choir had been rebuilt, work having been interrupted by feudal disputes and the Hundred Years' War, for Beauvais was in the front line in the battles fought by the king of France against the English and their Burgundian allies. The transept was begun in 1500, the north façade being finished in 1537, the southern in 1548. Then in 1568 the architect, Jean Vast, imprudently built on the pillars forming the cross of the transept a spire 490 feet high: but those on the west were inadequately buttressed and after five years the spire collapsed. Although repairs were completed by 1576 the cathedral never had a nave and the spire was never replaced.

But even in its present state, St Pierre is an awe-inspiring example of the extreme possibilities of Gothic art, the vertical lines of the interior reinforcing the soaring height of the pillars to give a wonderful impression of lightness. Of the two lateral façades of the 16th century, that on the south is the richer in detail. Other features are the ornately sculptured south portal built between 1500 and 1548, the 13th century stained glass windows, the great rose window in the transept, some Beauvais tapestries based on drawings by Raphael and the astronomical clock, which indicates the movements of the planets and tides and strikes the hours from noon until five.

That the plan for the cathedral was on such a grandiose scale was due to the vaunting ambitions of the powerful Prince-Bishops of Beauvais, who controlled no less than 1,000 feudal fiefs. Some of the bishops were highly articulate men, like Juvenal des Ursins, who wrote an eloquent account of the region during the Hundred Years War. Another, apparently less righteous, was Pierre Cauchon who sentenced Joan of Arc to the stake and was denounced by the townsfolk for his traitorous dealings with the Burgundians and the English. One of the most stirring events in which Beauvais was involved during this period occurred in 1472 when Charles the Bold, Duke of Burgundy, besieged the town with 80,000 troops. Only lightly garrisoned, Beauvais resisted the siege encouraged by a woman, Jeanne Laine, who, arming herself with an axe, drove off the Burgundians attempting to enter the town through a breach in the walls. Her bravery and the town's loyalty to the French crown, then worn by Louis XI, has been celebrated on the last Sunday in June ever since. A procession of people in medieval dress in which women take precedence over men comes to an end in the Place de l'Hotel de Ville where, beneath the statue of Jeanne Hachetée, as The Heroine later became known, the Fête de l'Assaut is re-enacted.

One Prince-Bishop of Beauvais decided to join the Third Crusade which led by Richard Coeur de Lion set off for the Holy Land in 1190. Before leaving, Bishop Philippe de Dreux ordered that from the tax on communes in his diocese an annual gift should be made to the lepers of the Maladrèrie St Lazaire he had founded outside the walls of the south of the town. In the Middle Ages Beauvais was ringed by fortifications maintained from the proceeds of a tax levied on all citizens and, like other fortified towns of the period, was congested and insanitary. Two ever-present dangers were fire and contagious disease. Of the second, leprosy — the "living death" introduced to France by knights returning from the Holy Land — was the enemy within which could wreak havoc in a community under siege. Strict laws were therefore introduced to protect the healthy. A man discovered to have leprosy was taken to the church where in front of the altar he was clothed in a red robe, measured for a coffin and given the last rites. He was then taken to the Maladrèrie, where he had to obey strictly enforced rules. With permission, he could go into the town, but he was not allowed to approach his wife, to enter a church, mill or bakery or to wash in streams or fountains. He had always to wear his red robe and to give warning of his approach. The Maladrèrie soon became rich from the gifts of property made to it, particularly by nobles setting off on the Crusades, but it subsequently fell into disorder and in the 17th century was suppressed, its land and buildings being put up for sale.

In the 18th century the people of Beauvais planted pretty avenues on the line of the ancient fortifications. And the ancient episcopal palace now houses the *musée départmentale* with its collection of wood carvings from the medieval houses destroyed in the bombing of 1940. It also contains some Beauvais tapestries, but the factory where these were produced was also destroyed in 1940 and has not been replaced. Founded in 1664 by Colbert to compete with the Flemish, the factory reached its apogee in the early 18th century, when the painter Oudry was the principal designer. A feature of the tapestry is its low warp, characterised by chain stitch in a horizontal pattern.

Beauvais grew up from a settlement established by the Bellovaci tribe in the marshes of the Therain, which flows south along the western edge of the Picard plain. An indication of the influence wielded in feudal times by the prince-bishops of Beauvais was the diocese of Beauvaisis, which extended into the plain to embrace Marseille on the northwest and Clermont on the east. The diocese was defended by numerous castles one of which, at Fontaine Lavaganne north of Marseille, still stands. Within the commune of Marseilles, an ancient settlement on the *route royale* to Paris, with its interesting 15th century church and chapel of the martyred saints, is the forest of Malmifait, a welcome splash of green in the otherwise highly cultivated plateau, its large and uniform undulations planted with fields of wheat and maize enclosing big agricultural villages, of which Luchy and Blicourt are typical.

*　　*　　*

At the time of the Romans the plateau was crossed by many roads (St Omer en Chaussée owes part of its name to one), some built for defence, others to serve the farmsteads (*villae rusticae*) then dotted about the countryside here as in other parts of Picardy; aerial sur-

103

veys reveal the foundations of more of them each year. Water is rare on the plateau but where valleys do exist they are wooded and green. From its source near Reuil the Breche meanders southeast along a pretty valley lined with trees, the river and its adjoining lakes and marshes rich in pike, trout, perch and eel. Beyond Etouy the Breche is joined by the Arrée, also picturesque where it passes through St Remy and Avrechy, then takes a more direct way along the eastern flank of the wooded massif of Clermont, a natural bastion of defence and the last point of Gallic resistance met by the legions of Julius Caesar in their second campaign against the Bellovaci in 51BC

Replacing earlier versions of wood, the first castle in stone on the summit of the massif was built by Baudouin de Claromonte in 1023. The harsh rule of this seigneur and his equally ruthless descendants came to an end in 1269, when saintly king Louis IX acquired the county of Clermont for his sixth son Robert, who adopted the name of his wife Beatrice de Bourbon. From this line descended the Bourbon kings of France. It was in the villages around Clermont a century or so later that the peasant uprising known as the Jacquerie first occurred. More than anything else, this was a desperate reaction to the misery created by the way the English waged the Hundred Years' War, their wanton destruction of the countryside, designed to weaken the power of the French king, hitting hardest at the peasants. The war officially came to an end after the battle of Châtillon in 1453, yet bands of English mercenaries continued to plunder a devastated Picardy, depopulated by famine and plague, its villages burned, its churches destroyed, its uncultivated fields a wilderness in which packs of wolves roamed and all traces of roads had disappeared.

Many of those who remained packed the fortified towns, where they had little enough food but were at least organised for defence. But the villages could offer no resistance to the invader. First came the English to loot and destroy, then in their wake arrived hungry French mercenaries who had to live and, since no arrangements were made to feed them, took from those they were supposed to defend. The nobles were called upon by the king to maintain companies of men at arms, added to the cost of which were the ransoms they themselves had to pay to the English after the disasters of Crécy and Poitiers and once more the peasants had to foot the bill. Finally, maddened by the wrongs done to them by foreigner and Frenchmen alike, the peasants exploded in anger, banding together spontaneously in the villages around Clermont and gaining new adherents all along the Therain valley. Each member of this loosely-knit organisation answered to the name of Jacques (a synonym for

104

A lake in Picardy

peasant), giving rise to the term Jacquèrie. They committed many
atrocities, certainly their declared purpose being to *detruire tous les
nobles et gentilshommes du monde.* But the movement lacked
discipline and leadership and after much bloodshed was repressed,
the 14th century chonicler Froissart reporting the killing of over
3,000 peasants in one day. Yet the Jacquèrie was to find new and
more effective expression in the frightful vengeance of the
Revolution of 1789.

   Crowning the massif, Clermont is centred on its historic *hotel de
ville* which, set in the ramparts, was a strongpoint in the town's

defence. Erected by Louis II of Bourbon in 1359, the building served a variety of purposes before being taken over by the municipality. From the Promenade du Châtellier, a pleasant walk at the foot of the ramparts dominated by the ruins of the ancient *donjon*, there are extensive views of the Picard plain. Nearby, the only fortified gate remaining is the Porte de Nointel which leads to the church of St Samson, built in the early 13th century and added to in the 15th and 16th, with its primitive vaulting above the choir and windows of stained glass from the 16th century workshops of Engrand Leprince of Beauvais. In the *hôtel de ville* is a museum-library containing books of the Ancien Regime, MSS, letters and medieval engravings. Clermont is crowded with Parisians most summer weekends; there is more likelihood of rubbing shoulders with local people at the Friday market.

On the northeastern edge of Clermont is the village which took the name of Jack Fitzjames, duke of Berwick and natural son of the English king James II, when he inherited it in 1704. James II fled to France with his son in 1689 and the "Bastard Royal" took up arms for his new country, an Englishman commanding Frenchmen who on one occasion won a battle fighting an English army commanded by a Frenchman. Fitz James (*fils de Jacques* or son of James) was killed at the battle of Phillipsburg in 1734. Dating from the 12th century, the church in the village had stained glass windows bearing the arms of England.

Beyond Clermont the Breche maintains a southerly course. In the meadows and cherry orchards east of the river are some charming villages, among them Catenoy, Labruyere and Cinqueux, each with an interesting small church. At Bois des Côtes near Nointel is evidence of a camp set up by the Romans during Caesar's second campaign. Verderonne, its pretty houses grouped round a castle, has a cultural tradition that goes back for centuries. The Atelier d'Art, a workshop for painters and sculptors, is open to visitors at weekends. Near Cinqueux are the marshes of Sacy le Grand, where the lush green of the surrounding poplars and willows creates a foil for the intensely blue water, the habitat of many species of birds.

On his wanderings through France Arthur Young, the 18th century agriculturist, was nothing if not critical of French ways. But for the duke of Liancourt, better known as La Rochefoucauld, with whom he stayed in 1787, he has nothing but praise. The rich and influential duke, an outstanding social and agricultural reformer, had established at Liancourt a model farm and the first arts and crafts school in France. The village has changed considerably since Arthur Young's day. In fact, it is now a small town crowded at weekends with Parisians staying in their *residences secondaires* that rise up on all sides, but the school established by the duke still thrives even if it has since been transferred to Chalons-sur-Marne. The duke's château has gone along with its fine gardens though the 15th century church contains some noble tombs.

West of the good fishing waters of the Breche are the 11-13th century churches of Ansacq, St Vaast, Hermes, St Felix and Lambronne. More remarkable, perhaps, is the church at Bury, with its arcaded nave built in 1140 and the capitals on its columns depicting scenes from daily life.

Bury is at the edge of the marsh-lined Therain; most of the village churches in the valley are built of the fine-grained stone of the region and still possess Romanesque naves and other 12th century features. La Neuville, with its ruined castle where the French king St Louis is said to have been born in 1225, has a church in transitional style with characteristics similar to those at Rue St Pierre and Agnetz.

La Neuville stands at the edge of the pretty Hez forest, covering some 6,000 acres, rich in game and bisected by many well marked roads and paths. It covers a plateau separating the valley of the Breche and the marshes of the Therain. At the foot of Mont Cesar west of the forest is a chapel and underground rooms, all that remain of the abbey of Froidmont founded in 1134.

Beyond Allonne, with its curious two-part church, the N1 highway veers to the right. But a more visually rewarding approach to Beauvais is on the old Route de Paris, which continues north to cross the Therain by the Pont de Paris. This is also the way to the Maladrerie St Lazaire, now part of a farm though the buildings that remain can be visited. These include a ruined romanesque church on the plan of a Latin cross, a 13th century rectangular building apparently used as a refectory with a dormitory above, and a superb grange with three naves divided by arcades beneath a vaulted timber-framed roof.

*   *   *

Forming a half-circle to the west of Beauvais, the three adjoining but geographically distinct *pays* of Bray, Vexin and Thelle await discovery by those content to travel on hedge-lined byways through unspoilt if only occasionally dramatic scenery to half-timbered villages clustered round parish churches often remarkable for their construction or decoration. In this gentle countryside well watered by rivers and streams the atmosphere is one of urbane good humour.

Its wooded landscape reminiscent of neighbouring Normandy, the *boutonnière* or depression of Bray northwest of Beauvais is bounded on the east by the Therain, which gurgles merrily south to provide some good fishing at Milly on the way. The country lanes that wind through this region, with its confused relief cloaked in rich vegetation husbanded by many small farms, reveal a different view at nearly every turn.

Beyond the splendid forest of Parc St Quentin, the clay soil around Savignies has been used to make ceramics of years, though the craft is now in decline. But at nearby Armentières and Vivier Danger you can still find at their wheels potters like Pierre Pissareff and Bouché-André, both of whom have set up modest museums in their workshops illustrating the development of local pottery.

Villages and towns in the Bray are often picturesque but few compete with Gerberoy, a pretty village on the west founded in 946 which has kept part of its fortified walls. In summer there are roses round every door. The village was often a pawn in Anglo-French rivalry and the little museum in the *mairie* gives some idea of its history.

Before the Revolution, abbeys wielded great temporal power in the Bray, most of them being founded in the 7th century on the initiative of St Ouen, bishop of Rouen. One of the most important was St Germer de Fly, near Gournay to the southwest, founded in 633 by St Germer, counsellor to the Carolingian king Dagobert I. Sacked in the 9th century by the Normans, the abbey was restored in 1030 but again pillaged and destroyed several times. Built in 1160 on the ruins of its 7th century predecessor, the abbey church illustrates in a remarkable way the progression from the Romanesque to the Gothic style. It adjoins the 13th century funeral chapel of Ste Chapelle, copied from its namesake in Paris and housing the tombstone of minor local nobles: Gerard d'Eragny (1236), Michel de Catenoy (1284) and Jean de Silly (1390). Remains of the abbey proper include a fortified gateway and a timber priory of the 16th century. One notable abbot of St Germer was Eustache, charged with the task of preaching the fourth Crusade in England. No one seems to know the reason for the suffix "de Fly". The little town built around the abbey wakes up from its usual torpor on Ascension Thursday, the day the Fête Guillenfosse is held.

At Villenbray (Ville-en-Bray) the stained glass in the chapel portrays a 9th century pilgrimage. Close by the ruined fort of Goulancourt, the church at nearby Senantes contains among other historic objects baptismal fonts of the 13th century. On the byway east of St Germer, the tiny village of Lalandelle, with its orientation table, borders the forest of Thelle in which there are oaks three centuries old. South of the forest is the village of La Bosse, so called from the hill (*bosse* or hump) on which its 15th century church is perched.

From Le Vaumain further south the road runs alongside the Aunette, crossing the stream near Trie-Château to enter the Vexin, named from the Velicasses tribe of the Belgae which lived there in primitive times. This limestone plateau sloping east-west and crossed by green valleys ends on the north in two successive escarpments, with an intermediary platform six or seven miles wide. Many places on the plateau are vantage points for immense panoramas. The landscape is an intimate mixture of woods and crops, with here and there big farmsteads built for defence round an inner courtyard. The need for these and for the line of fortresses that once marched north from Trie came about because the Epte valley on the west formed from the 9th to the 13th centuries the frontier between the rival states of Normandy and France.

In the hope of converting the ferocious Norman warriors into peaceful settlers Charles the Simple, king of the Franks, gave their chief Rollo in 911 all the territory between the sea and the rivers Andelle and Epte. This arrangement, which cut the Vexin in two, was confirmed by the treaty of Gerberoy, signed in 946 by Louis IV and Richard I, duke of Normandy. But the Normans, far from remaining peaceful, constantly tried to expand their territory on the east at the expense of the Franks, making it necessary to build the fortresses along the right bank of the Epte. These were spaced some distance apart since the river was then flanked by marshes making it difficult to cross. Charged with the defence of the Vexin Français were the counts of Vexin, a dynasty founded by Gautier I which survived until the region was annexed by the French king in 1076.

The first of the long series of disputes between the English and French kings which marked most of the Middle Ages was the Normans' claim to this, the French part of the Vexin. Only a year after being crowned at Westminster, in 1067, William the Conqueror re-iterated the claim, and it was here, when he invaded the region 20 years later, that he met his death.

Some of the castles along the banks of the Epte were dismantled on the order of Richelieu. Others were restored and altered, like that at Trie Château — first built in the 11th century to defend the French half of the Vexin — where the last duke of Condé gave refuge to Jean-Jacques Rousseau and enough peace of mind to enable him to finish writing his Confessions. In the main street nearby is the most ancient town hall in France, built in 1160 and still retaining its Romanesque windows. More interesting, perhaps, is the chateau at Alincourt near Parnes, built in the 15th century by Pierre Legendre, treasurer to

Charles VIII, and acquired in 1764 by the marquis de Vallière, whose descendants still live there surrounded by a rich collection of furniture and tapestries of the period.

But the Vexin is notable less for its castles than for its churches, which occupy an important place in the history of religious architecture in France. Few could fail to be charmed by the Romanesque façade of the church at the picturesque village of Trie Château, restored by Viollet-le-Duc. Nearby reached by a flight of steps and flanked by a massive tower, is the 16th century church at Chaumont, on the right bank of the Troesne below the Vexin 'cliff' dominating the Thelle region; it incorporates some fine vaulting and has a notable unity of style. Its counterpart at Parnes has a beautiful 16th century decorated portal, and that at Montjavoult, from where there are extensive views, is equally decorative but contained within a sunken panel. At Montagny, dominated on the east by the Mont de Serans, one of the highest points in the Vexin, is a pretty church of the 12th and 13th centuries. There is one of the same period at Reilly, a *village fleuri* on the right bank of the Reveillon, and yet another at Boury, a delightful village with a pretty château built in 1685 by Mansart for the local marquis. But there are many other churches and flower-decked villages in the Vexin that repay discovery.

Meru, on the N327 south of Beauvais, is the gateway to the *pays* of Thelle, here an open cultivated plain which rises imperceptibly to a point in the north even higher than the Vexin plateau. The hamlet of Angleterre to the right of the main road is supposed to occupy the site of a camp set up by the English during the Hundred Years' War. Beyond its northern neighbour Laboissière, the height gained becomes noticeable for the first time, the road north to Coudray running along the edge of high ground to Neuville, on the crest. From there, the view extends in a wide arc to take in the whole of Beauvais and its green surroundings.

* * *

Three towns on popular routes through eastern Picardy merit a closer look than many tourists give them, for each has a magnificent cathedral and other interesting features to make even a brief halt rewarding. The history of Soissons, Noyon and St Quentin is closely linked with that of Picardy and though all were sadly damaged in recent wars they display many relics of a long and varied past.

One of the oldest settlements in France, Soissons was destined by its geographical location to be attacked by any invader from the

Saint Jean des Vignes, the Abbey Church, Soissons

north. Second most important town in Belgian Gaul, the place where Clovis defeated the Roman legions in 486 and the cradle of the French monarchy when in 511 it became the capital of Neustria under Charlemagne, it witnessed the crowning of Pepin the Short at the abbey of St Medard in 752 and the defeat of Charles the Simple outside its walls in 923. Frequently under siege in the Middle Ages, notably by the English during the Hundred Years' War, it was overrun by the Prussians in 1870 and several times occupied by the Germans in the 1914-18 war.

Not far from the main shopping street of Rue St Martin, the cathedral of St Gervais and St Protais is a fine Gothic building mainly of the 13th century, though the façade, flanked by two square towers, was modified in the 18th. The oldest and most beautiful part of the vast interior is the south transept, with its fine cross vaulting and graceful arcades. South of the cathedral, only the flamboyant façade and openwork spires remain of the abbey church of St Jean des Vignes, founded in 1076 and demolished by imperial decree in 1805. Other parts of the Augustinian abbey which have survived include a magnificent vaulted cellar, fragments of a large and small cloister and an elegant refectory divided into two naves by slender pillars. To the north of the cathedral, the ruined 12th century abbey of St Leger retains a vaulted Romanesque crypt, chapter house and two galleries of a cloister. The abbey houses the municipal museum, with its archeological collections from Gallo-Roman to medieval times. On the right bank of the Aisne, beyond the suburb of St Vaast, are the mostly subterranean remains of the once-powerful abbey of St Medard which include a 9th century crypt consisting of a central gallery flanked on the east by seven chapels and on the west by three vaulted sepulchres housing the tomb of the saint and those of the founders, the Merovingian kings Clotaire and Sigebert.

Soissons is supposed to get its name from its trade in *soissons* (beans) but a more likely explanation is Suessiona, the title the Romans gave it as the second capital of Belgica.

Until 1917 Noyon was the nearest German-occupied town to Paris, a mere 65 miles away. The statesman Clemenceau rammed the point home to his countrymen when he made the oft-quoted remark "*Messieurs les Allemands sont encore à Noyon.*" It is religion, not war that looms large in the history of Noyon, yet the small town on the Oise is one of the most cheerful. Here Gerard Calvin settled in 1480 and within a few years became treasurer of the diocese. His son Jean, born July 10 1509, left Noyon in 1521 to study at Paris, Orleans and Bourges, returning to his parents' home only for short visits. Gerard Calvin's handling of the finances of the diocese resulted in his

Library of the Cathedral, Noyon

excommunication, a fact which probably more than any other prompted his famous son, whose dogmatism and critical sense are traits typical of the Picard character, to become the founder of Protestantism.

On view in the cathedral of Notre Dame, a building of sober power and the fifth church to be erected on the site, are the bones of St Eloi, the bishop of Noyon who died in 659. Completed at the end of the 12th century, the cathedral combines the simple strength of Romanesque with the bold elegance of Gothic, the severe lines of the façade contrasting with the lightness and decoration of the interior. Inside, one piece of statuary commemorates Guillaume Bovillé, counsellor to Charles VII and doyen of the chapter of Noyon from 1447 to 1476. He was ordered by the king to head an inquiry into the trial of Joan of Arc, the French heroine being rehabilitated at Rouen as a result in 1456. One of the canonical dependencies that still surrounded the cathedral is the chapter library, a 16th century wooden building in which the most prized possession is the 9th century *evangélaire* of Morienval. Local history is portrayed in the municipal museum and a reconstruction of Calvin's house contains documents and books showing the development of his doctrine.

Noyon, centred on a pretty Renaissance *hôtel de ville* with stepped gables and with its town walls replaced by a circular boulevard in 1830, is surrounded by attractive wooded scenery. At the edge of a forest south of the town is the Cistercian abbey of Ourscamp, founded in a loop of the Oise by St Bernard in 1129 and enlarged in the 18th century. The monastic infirmary, now a chapel, dates from 1240 and is divided into three naves by two rows of columns; below each of the small arched windows in the lateral naves was placed the bed of an invalid. The way to the infirmary leads past the ruins of the huge 13th century abbey church. In 1807 Radix of Ste Foy bought the abbey buildings, converting the monastery into a country retreat and partly demolishing the church to create a romantic ruin in his park.

Astride the Somme at the eastern edge of the fertile Vermandois plain, St Quentin has an attractive centre undiscovered by many travellers put off by the industry on the left bank of the river and the futuristic residential quarter on the north. The town was reduced almost to ruins when it was occupied by the Germans for the whole of the 1914-18 war, yet among its quiet central streets three important buildings have survived: the delightful 15th century town hall, the huge basilica begun in the 13th century and completed in the 15th and the Lecuyer museum with its superb collection of pastels by the 18th century portrait artist Maurice Quentin de la Tour. Also in the

Ruins of the Abbey, Ourscamp

centre is the Champs Élysées park, with its wooded walks. To the southeast is the Etang de l'Isle, a lake formed by the Somme near the point where the road to Laon crosses the river; from the beach at the lakeside there are impressive views of the town.

St Quentin owes much of its present importance to the martyr from whom it takes its name. A modest Gallo-Roman settlement on the Somme when Quintinius, the brother of a Roman senator of Laon and an evangelising Christian was captured and killed by the Gauls in 287 on the spot now marked by the basilica, it quickly became a place of pilgrimage. In feudal times as now prosperous from its trade in textiles, it was the scene in 1557 of the celebrated siege by the invading Spaniards, an event recalled by a monument in the town hall square. A few years later, in 1560, St Quentin formed part of the dowry of Mary Queen of Scots.

The Renaissance town hall has a flamboyant façade of great delicacy, consisting of a covered gallery of seven arcades decorated with sculpture, a first floor with nine windows and above a balustrade in which are set three rose windows, the whole topped by a campanile housing a 30-bell carillon. Each of the tall columns inside the nearby basilica, with its beautiful choir and 9th century crypt containing the tomb of the martyr, bears the mark of a cavity the Germans filled with dynamite and wired to booby traps before they evacuated the town in 1918. The French troops who entered the church on the heels of the Germans were fortunately aware of the danger and defused the charges.

The 90 pastels by la Tour, born at St Quentin in 1704, represent most of his life's work and form a remarkable record of the personalities of French society in the 18th century. The portraits, of considerable psychological depth, are a subtle revelation of the sitter's character and temperament, yet la Tour was very much a man of his time and well aware of the need for flattery. His style, a symphony of greys, derives largely from the Dutch artist Van Dyck. He became rich and in later life returned to St Quentin, where he died in 1788 on the eve of the French Revolution.

7
THE VALOIS

One of the noblest and most gracious regions of France, the limestone plateau of the Valois is cloaked in great forests, furrowed by deep valleys, decorated with elegant châteaux and bathed in a diaphanous light which gives its many scenic views the quality of an impressionist painting. Although the forests cover large areas of the plateau, saved from monotony by hills and sandy bluffs, the fertile soil in the clearings is renowned for its wheat and many small towns set in the pastel-tinted landscape are rural markets still.

From the earliest times, when it formed the heart of the Capet dynasty, the Valois was at the centre of the French monarchs' slow and laborious struggle to build a nation from a handful of provinces. Subsequently, its ducal family produced the Valois kings, whose ascent to the throne in 1328 was closely followed by the opening of the Hundred Years' War, when the English ravaged the region despite the fortresses built to defend it. From François I onwards, other kings built castles here for pleasure, where they staged brilliant courts or set off for the hunt. But the Valois is also rich in Romanesque and Gothic architecture in the form of great cathedrals and homely parish churches, as it is in aristocratic cities and pretty villages. Here the grand and the modest blend happily together, reflecting the region's mellow character, as much Ile-de-France as it is Picard.

A tour of the Valois should begin at forest-ringed Senlis, an ancient Gallo-Roman town of great charm. An aerial view shows that it consists of concentric rings of buildings following the line of the walls that enclosed it in medieval times. The main façade of the Gothic cathedral, dedicated in 1191, is decorated with two splendid tympanums and the interior is remarkable for its lightness and balance. A favourite town of the dukes of Valois and later of many kings, Senlis retains its Château Royal in which Hugh Capet was elected king in 987 and Henry V of England married Catherine of France; an 18th century extension houses a hunting museum unique of its kind. Flanked by houses with vaulted cellars and enclosed courtyards, some of the ancient streets bear names whose origin is lost in time; others, displaying the names of crafts, date from the 14th century, when the town spilled out beyond its ramparts. On the western edge of Senlis are the remains of a sunken Roman arena that once seated 10,000 people.

Northeast of Senlis along the little road through the forest is the village of Aumont, where the French writer Henri Barbusse, a man of considerable talent born of an English mother, lived until his death in 1935. His house, the Villa Sylvie, is now an intimate little museum illustrating his life and work.

Elegant Chantilly may now be celebrated more for its horse racing — over 4,000 thoroughbreds are trained in the district — than for its lace or its cream whipped to fluffy lightness, but its romantic chateau is unlikely ever to be left out of account. Built on two islands in a lake formed by the Nonette stream, the castle is actually two in one, the 16th century Petit Château and the 19th century Grand Château, tastefully linked together. Inside is the Condé museum, with magnificent paintings, sculpture and tapestries displayed in panelled rooms,

Château de Chantilly

an outstanding 15th century illuminated manuscript *Les Tres Riches Heures du Duc de Berry* consisting of twelve panels depicting the months of the year, and a superb collection of miniatures by the French painter Fouquet. Jewels on view include the great pink nine-carat diamond known as Le Grand Condé, named like the museum after its ducal owners who in 1719 commissioned the stone stables or Grandes Ecuries, which house 240 horses and are separated from the château by a park designed by Le Notre. Nearby is the famous race-course, one of the prettiest in Europe. Earlier and later owners of Chantilly were the Connetable of Montmorency, in the 16th century holder of power under six successive kings, and the Duc d'Aumale, who lived part of his life at Twickenham on the Thames and who in the late 19th century bequeathed the château and its contents to the French nation.

West of Chantilly, Gouvieux stands on the right bank of the Nonette at the edge of the forest of Lys close by one of the prettiest stretches of the Oise. Beyond Lamorlaye, *Morlacum* (lakeland) in Roman times, is Coye la Fôret, a pleasant village on the Theve near the high plateau of Bruyeres, from which there are beautiful forest views. A scenic road follows the north bank of the Theve to Commelles, where the river forms elongated lakes which reflect the romantically situated château de la Reine Blanche, a pseudo-Gothic hunting lodge built for the duke of Bourbon in 1826; legend has it that the "White Queen" Blanche of Navarre, wife of Philippe de Valois, built a castle on the spot in 1350.

*   *   *

At the villages of Thiers the road emerges from the forest of Chantilly to enter that of Ermenonville, consisting mostly of oaks and pines, and arrive at Mortefontaine, where Joseph Bonaparte possessed a vast domain. At the edge of the village is the Parc Vallière which provided the inspiration for many of Corot's paintings. In a pretty park nearby are the ruins of the beautiful Gothic church and chapel of the Cistercian abbey of Chaalis, founded in 1136. They adjoin a building called "the château" which is in fact the only completed part (the northern logis) of a vast quadrangle planned by the abbot a few years before the French Revolution. The simply styled and perfectly proportioned logis, designed by Jean Aubert, architect of the Grandes Écuries at Chantilly, houses a museum containing many works of art. Beyond the abbey gate is the curious Mer de

119

Sable, a sea of sand with a whiteness which contrasts sharply with the lush green of the surrounding woodlands.

The park enclosing the château of Ermenoville, created by the marquis of Girardin in 1766, was one of the earliest gardens in France in the informal English style. His idea, a rather puerile one, was to 'embellish nature'; make-believe ruins (*fabriques*) designed to appeal to the emotions of the beholder are supplemented by panels bearing quotations from famous philosophers. Jean-Jacques Rousseau, whom Girardin admired to a fanatical degree, died while a guest of the marquis in 1778 and was buried on a tiny poplar-shaded island in the park, though his body was later moved to the Parthenon in Paris. The main street of the village passes in front of the pretty château, built for Girardin in 1776. On a farm north of Chaalis abbey is the impressive rectangular keep and circular walls of the ruined castle of Montépilloy, built by the Bouteiller family of Senlis, cup-bearers at the court of the first Capet kings.

On the western edge of the Retz forest, Crépy is a picturesque old town on a spur overlooking two valleys which retains its majestic ramparts on the east, the line of the fortifications being continued by attractive walks. Some medieval houses still exist, as does the *hôtel de ville* of 1537 and the church set in the walls in the 12th century and dedicated to a contemporary martyr, Thomas à Becket. The keep of the 12th century ducal castle houses a museum of folklore and archery, a traditional Valois sport still popular in the region. In the Middle Ages the capital of the duchy of Valois, Crépy was several times sacked by the English during the Hundred Years' War.

The English were less successful in their attacks on the little town of Ferté Milon astride the Oureq, defended as it was by a huge fortress in an impregnable position high above the valley. Bas reliefs depicting the crowning of the Virgin decorate the façade of the castle, built by Louis of Orleans in the early 15th century to protect the eastern flank of the Valois plateau and now a forlorn and empty shell. In the town, a statue reminds the visitor that this is the birthplace of the 17th century dramatist Jean Racine. Present-day tourists admire, as he probably did, the beautiful stained glass windows of the little Renaissance church of St Nicolas, with its watch tower and fortified belfry. A drive south along the pretty Ourcq valley reveals hidden lakes, the *commanderie* of Montigny-Allier and the keep of the castle at Crouy.

To one side of the fast road through the forest from Ferté Milon to Villers Cotterêts lies the 14th century Chartreuse of Bourgfontaine, on the other the delightful village of Oigny, and both demand to be seen.

Museum of Crépy-en-Valois

Villers Cotterêts takes its name from the vast forest that encloses it on the north, south and east, referred to in medieval French as *cot*, hence Cot-de-Retz, though an alternative version is Villa-à-coté-de-Retz. Occupying the summit of the plateau and enclosing the picturesque valley of the Automne, the forest consists mostly of oak trees, some of which reach a height of 130 feet. It shelters a variety of big and small game, including deer — a real hazard for motorists driving on the forest roads.

However it acquired its name, Villers grew up round a hunting lodge built in the 10th century by the dukes of Valois which François I replaced in 1535 by a more comfortable château designed for him by Jacques and Guillaume le Breton. It was from the château, his favourite residence, that François I ordered in 1539 that French should replace Latin on all official documents and that every parish should keep a register of births, marriages and deaths, thereby establishing the basis of a civil state in France. The king came to Villers to hunt in the forest, most hilly and picturesque on the north. What little there is to see in the château, under Napoleon I a hospice for beggars and now a home for retired people, dates from the period of Fra-

121

Château of Villers-Cotterêts

nçois I — the grand staircase displaying the king's salamander emblem and the richly decorated state rooms. Behind the castle is a park, once the royal gardens, where anyone can now walk freely.

The town may have owed its origins to the château but its subsequent development was due to various administrative offices being established there on the insistence of the dukes of Orleans, whose favourite residence it was. In the 17th and 18th centuries, when the average rate of travel was 25 kilometres a day, it also prospered because it was the last staging post between Paris and Soissons on the road to the north, its 35 "*hostelleryes*" catering for all sorts of travellers. Wood merchants put up at the Coq, *les petites gens à pied* at the Cheval Blanc, the chartreux of Bourgfontaine at the St Nicolas, kings and nobles at the Croix d'Or and l'Epee Royale, and those thirsting for wine, song and the solace of a woman's bed at the Croix Rouge, which was authorised to remain open for two hours after curfew and where there were six *serveuses* of easy virtue. The only one of these relais to have survived is the Croix d'Or, now known as the Regent. Though modernised, it retains some features of the period, not least its rooms named after some of the famous people who stayed there.

Villers Cotterêts was the home town of Alexandre Dumas, the 19th century writer of romantic novels and plays, his father and his grandfather, a general of Napoleon who fell out of favour for disagreeing with the emperor. In the street named after the son is a small museum devoted to all three men.

During the Revolution the wise Lavoisier of Villers was put to death with the words "*La Republique n'a pas besoin de savants*". Nor, apparently, did it have need of religious institutions, all of which were suppressed — their properties at best sold to private buyers, at worst razed to the ground like the Cistercian abbey of Longpont, the melancholy ruins of which stand at the eastern edge of the Retz forest. Founded by St Bernard and dedicated in the presence of St Louis and Blanche of Castille in 1227, they abbey housed 300 monks, of whose former cemetery not a trace remains. All that is left of the abbey is part of the 12th century church, the cloister and the circular *chauffoir* with its central chimney — the only room in which the monks were allowed to warm themselves in winter, and then only for a few minutes each day. Longpont is named from the long bridge the monks built when reclaiming marshes nearby. They also created from the Savière river running through the abbey grounds a lake they stocked with fish, their staple food, supplemented by vegetables, bread and honey (the comb they used to make candles). They drank beer and on special occasions wine.

On the far side of the Retz forest, to the west, is Vez, the centre of the *pagus vadensis*, the nucleus of the Valois. High above the wooded Automne valley, the tiny village possesses two remarkable buildings, the 12th century church of St Martin, with its beautiful choir, timber-roofed nave and ancient wooden statues, and the well preserved castle, rebuilt at the end of the 14th century by Louis of Orleans, which has a central pentagonal keep guarded by five corbelled towers and in the courtyard a chapel containing a museum of the Valois.

Enclosed in a deep valley, the small Romanesque abbey church of Morienval dating from 1125 is unusual in having three belfries, two of which flank the choir. It is even more unusual in that it was the first church in Europe to incorporate the *ogivale croisée* or crossed pointed arch, which heralded the Gothic style and revolutionised church building in the West. One constructional advantage of cross vaulting was that it allowed walls to be thinner, enabling them to be opened up with windows. Inside are the tombstones of the abbesses of Morienval and the effigy of the knight Florent de Viri of Hangest on the Somme, protector of the abbey, who died on the Third Crusade during the siege of Acre in 1191.

Easily reached from nearby Orrouy are the important Gallo-Roman ruins of Champlieu, a *vicus sanctuaire* — combining a rest house for travellers, a market and a place of worship — established

Church at Morienval

Arches at Morienval

Palace of Louis XV, Compiègne

beside the Roman road that linked Senlis and Soissons. The ruins, still being excavated, are of a temple dedicated to Apollo, a theatre seating 4,000 and thermal baths. Catacombs where some of the first Christians held their services have also been discovered nearby.

Champlieu is at the southern edge of the extensive Compiègne forest, sixty miles round and a blaze of yellows, reds and browns in autumn. Most hilly in the east and south, it was pierced in the 12th century only by winding paths. François I was the first to open up the forest to aid the hunt, cutting eight roads radiating from the Puits du Roi to the perimeter. Louis XV created an additional network on a geometric plan designed by the architect Gabriel. Around the Puits de Roi the network forms three polygons, the Octagonet, Little Octagon and the Big Octagon. To make hunting in the forest easier, the space between the roads is triangular, enabling a horseman at the apex to see any deer leaving one enclosure for another.

Lake at Pierrefonds

In the forest is the charming village of St Jean aux Bois, which owes its origin to a Benedictine abbey founded in 1152 by Adelaide, widow of Louis VI. The abbey church, with its high vaulted nave, is notable for its purity of style. Vieux Moulin, another forest village, is dominated on the north by the elongated plateau of Mont St Marc. In a sumptuous setting nearby, the chalet of the Empress Eugenie overlooks the lakes of St Pierre, above which is another *mont* with a ruined church and a miraculous fountain, the water from which was said to cure sterility. To the north in a loop of the Oise is the Clairière where the armistice was signed by the Germans on November 11 1918. The site is marked by the railway carriage of Marshal Foch in which the signing took place and a building housing stereoscopic photographs of the fighting and relics of the war.

Pierrefonds surrounds a lake at the foot of the splendid reconstruction by Viollet le Duc of a feudal castle built in 1400. A perfect example of medieval military architecture, it forms a square isolated on three sides by escarpments and on the fourth by a moat, the main

128

Château of Raray

façade being protected by a tower at each corner and another in the centre. Together with the duchy of Valois, the castle was given in 1392 by Charles VI to his brother Louis of Orleans, who completed the original structure in 1407. But it was out of date before it was built. Besieged in 1413, it was put to the torch by the retreating Count of St Pol. Dismantled by Louis XIII in 1617, the castle was bought in 1813 by Napoleon I for 2,950 francs, and in 1857 Napoleon III engaged Viollet-le-Duc to restore it. The reconstruction, begun by le Duc but finally completed by other architects in 1884, draws a parallel in the decoration of the knights hall and other parts of the interior between Napoleon III and his court and the figures of the Arthurian legends.

There are around 300 crossroads in the forest, each displaying a direction sign at the height of a man on horseback, with red arrows pointing to Compiègne. So the visiting motorist is unlikely to repeat the experience of the dauphin Philippe Auguste who, as a young man, was lost in the forest for two days without food.

The severely-styled palace of Compiègne, built by Louis XV to plans drawn up by Gabriel, is one of the most grandiose of the Ancien Regime. In the somewhat lifeless building, Napoleon married Marie Louise and each autumn Napoleon Bonaparte and the empress Eugenie staged a brilliant court. Open to visitors are rooms of the First and Second Empire, furnished in the style of the period, and a museum illustrating the history of transport. The centre of the town is the square in which a statue of Joan of Arc is overlooked by the pretty 16th century town hall; three carved wooden figures (the Picantins) appear when the bell in its tower sounds the quarter hours. The hôtel de ville houses an extensive collection of lead soldiers from Vercingetorix to General de Gaulle, and the Hotel de Songeons another of antique vases. Compiègne's old ramparts still stand, as does the tower where Joan of Arc is said to have been imprisoned after her capture by the Burgundians at nearby Margny in 1430.

Prisoners whose jailers were just as brutal as Joan's departed more recently from Royallieu, on the Paris road out of Compiègne. Here from 1941 the Germans assembled deportees from Picardy and other parts of France. The first train left the adjoining marshalling yards on April 25 1941 for Buchenwald, the last on August 8 1944 for Weimar. In between over 200 fully-packed trains departed from Royallieu for these and other concentration camps. A plaque erected by the roadside recalls this murderous traffic.

A worthwhile excursion from Verberie, on the left bank of the Oise and offering good fishing, is south to the château of Raray, famous for its exterior perspective of decorative sculpture devoted to the hunt and for its park where Cocteau made the film *La Belle et la Bête*. Pontpoint, where the Romanesque church has a belfry of several storeys, is at the northern edge of the Halatte forest, dominated by Mont Pagnotte and shaded by tall beechwoods which in spring are carpeted with wild flowers.

8
LAON AND THE LAONNAIS

Architecture in which spiritual and temporal power found its highest expression in the Middle Ages is much in evidence in Laon, in the pretty Laonnois occupying a semi-circular area to the south and in the oak and beech forest of St Gobain-Coucy adjoining it on the west.

Crowning an isolated hill visible for thirty miles round, the ancient quarter of Laon generates a truly medieval atmosphere, due not only to such monuments as the magnificent Notre-Dame cathedral, the chapel of the Templars and the fortified gates set in the ancient ramparts, but also to the other historic buildings in its narrow winding streets, among them the royal abbey of St Jean housing the prefecture, the bishops' palace, now the courts of justice, and the citadel built by Henri IV from which the town is administered.

A fortified encampment in Gallo-Roman times, Laon was made a bishopric in the 5th century by St Remi, archbishop of Reims. Under the last Carolingian kings the capital of France and an impregnable royal residence, it was adopted by Bertha, mother of Charlemagne, then by Charles the Bald, Louis IV and Louis V. By the 11th century it had become the acknowledged capital of Upper Picardy and a renowned centre of religious and intellectual influence, its hostelries regularly patronised by pilgrims on their way to St James of Compostella in Spain and its school of philosophy attended by students from all over Europe eager to hear the lectures of Anselm and Raoul de Laon.

Dominating the town is the imposing mass of the cathedral, the first on this scale in France. A superb example of pure Romano-Gothic built between 1155 and 1225, it has served as a model for many other churches elsewhere. Of its five towers, the tallest are those on the north and south, each nearly 200 feet high. The two tiered towers on the west façade, an architectural wonder, are the smallest; these, bearing the sculptured heads of oxen, recall the legend that when a cart laden with stone for the building was unable to climb the hill an ox mysteriously appeared to help, vanishing when the load reached the top. More likely, oxen were used to drag the stone to the site and by representing them the architect is acknowledging that without their aid the church could not have been built. Anyone courageous enough to climb the winding stairs inside one of the towers can enjoy an immense view of the surrounding country.

Laon Cathedral

Pillars of Laon Cathedral

    Incorporating a huge rose window, the west façade is famous for its recessed and elegantly proportioned portals surmounted by sculptured tympanums depicting the Creation and the liberal arts. The vast arcaded nave flanked by beautiful side chapels is supported by tastefully grouped pillars and behind the choir are three lancet windows containing some historic stained glass. One of the tall pillars near the choir, of a single piece of stone, reverberates like a tuning fork when struck with the hand. It indicates the mastery of medieval masons, who took care to place the stone used in a building in exactly the same stress position it occupied when quarried.

    Gautier of Mortagne initiated the building of the cathedral but the most admired of the all-powerful bishops of Laon was Barthelemy de Jur who in his episcopat of nearly forty years founded almost as many abbeys in the Laonnois and elsewhere. Laon was one of the first towns to claim its municipal liberty and one of the last to obtain it. Incensed by the refusal of the oppressive bishop Gaudry to listen to their demands, the citizens rose up in 1112 and not only put him to death but also set fire to his palace. The King of France intervened only to provoke more massacres and it was not until 1128 that order was restored.

Entered from the cathedral parvis is the *Salle Gothique*, an underground hall used as a leper hospital in the 13th century. From the hall a passage enabled the lepers to enter the church without coming into contact with the healthy. Each September the town recreates its feudal past with the Medieval Hours festival, when the hall is used as a tavern.

Temporal and spiritual power combined most comfortably in the Middle Ages on the consciences of warrior monks like the Knights Templars, an order founded in 1118 at Jerusalem during the First Crusade by a group of nobles headed by Hugues de Payns, a cousin of St Bernard. Based on the Cistercian ideals of obedience and poverty and the protection of pilgrims and sacred places in the Holy Land, the order was organised in *commanderies* or communitites throughout France. In the garden of the municipal museum at Laon is the only reminder of the *commanderie* established in the town, a vaulted funeral chapel built to an octagonal plan in 1128. The chapel contains the 14th century effigy of Guillaume, a native of Harcigny in the Thiérache and doctor to the mad king Charles VI, who died at the age of ninety after stipulating that his body should be exhumed a year after his death and then reproduced in sculpture. The realistic effigy of his skeleton, showing how its hair and nails had continued to grow in the tomb, set a fashion very popular in the 15th and 16th centuries.

Beside the Paris road is the church of the abbey of St Martin built in 1124 on land given by the lord of Coucy, whose effigy it contains. Near the church is a military hospital converted from property formerly belonging to the abbey, with a walled garden enclosing a stone pavilion called ironically the "*Vide Bouteille*" or Empty Bottle in which the monks poured wine for their guests.

Miles of pleasant walks have been created at the foot of the 13th century ramparts in which were once set nine fortified gates: now only those of Ardon, Chenizelles and Soissons remain. From the Chenizelles gate a steep and picturesque street leads to the *bibliotheque* housing the personal books of Charles the Bald and many relics from the ruined abbeys of the Laonnois.

Near the Boetien marshes east of Laon is the flamboyant Gothic basilica of Notre Dame de Liesse, built to shelter the miraculous statue of the black Virgin. Legend has it that three knights from the region were taken prisoner by the sultan of Cairo while on a Crusade to the Holy Land. The sultan sent his daughter Ismery to convert them to the Islamic faith but when a wooden statue of the Virgin miraculously materialised in the prison she herself became a Christian and with the knights and the statue was transported to the spot now covered by the basilica. Venerated from the 12th century, the statue was burned during the wave of anti-religious feeling that marked the Revolution, the one replacing it being sculptured in 1857. In the basilica, decorated with many *ex votos*, is a chapel dedicated to St Louis, one of the many kings who came to worship at Liesse. Others were Henri II, François II and Charles IX, who during their pilgrimage stayed at the nearby Renaissance château of Marchais as guests of Charles of Lorraine, archbishop of Reims.

In the green and wooded farmland of the Laonnois beyond Coucy les Eppes are many charming parish churches built in the 12th and 13th centuries. The church at Vorges, like its modest counterpart at Presles, was fortified during the Hundred Years' War. That at Nouvion-le-Vineux has a great Romanesque belfry of three storeys, primitive Gothic vaulting in the nave and in the porch the tombstone of the Irishman Jean Offarelle (O'Farrell), mayor of the village in the 19th century. Most beautiful is the church at Urcel, a Romanesque building with an unusual frieze below the roof of the nave and sculptured capitals on the pillars supporting it. The delightful village of Mons en Laonnois has a church on the plan of a Greek cross and interesting *creuttes* or troglodyte cave dwellings nearby. There are other notable churches at Bruyeres and Royaucourt.

Nouvion le Vineux acquired the suffix to its name during the Middle Ages, when the vineyards covering every south-facing slope in the Laonnois produced the holy *Gout d'Or* wine for most of the churches in France. The flourishing wine trade then established with England and the countries of the north lasted until the 17th century, and still to be seen in the area are some pretty *vendangeoirs*, not unlike a farm, where the grapes were pressed and the wine fermented.

Along the crest of the limestone cliff separating the Aisne and Ailette valleys in the southern Laonnois runs the *Chemin des Dames*. This ancient ridge-top road, which gives extensive views of wooded country, takes its name from the Mesdames or daughters of Louis XV, who regularly bumped along it in their carriage when visiting their maid of honour the duchess of Narbonne at the Château de la Bove, now a lonely ruin near the eastern end of the highway. Military cemeteries flank the road, for it was in the front line for the whole of the 1914-18 war. Many of the men buried in the cemeteries marked by the tricolour were killed in General Nivelle's abortive

Cavern of the Dragon Museum on the Chemin des Dames

attack of April 1917 which for the gain of a few yards of ground cost the French army 30,000 dead and 85,000 wounded, these terrible losses so lowering the survivors' morale that many of them refused to leave their trenches. Discipline was restored by the simple and ruthless expedient of 'decimation' taking one man in ten from the ranks of the mutineers and putting them before a firing squad.

Near Cerny and recognisable by the French 75 and German 77

guns above its entrance is the *Caverne du Dragon*, an underground quarry covering an area no less than five acres from which came the stone used to build the cathedral of Laon and the churches of the Laonnois. Occupied for most of the war by the Germans, the cavern acquired its name because it then had seven entrances on the south and each spat fire from the machine guns guarding them, a phenomenon recalling the seven-headed mythological dragon Hydra. Used as a forward command post and an arsenal, it housed 600 men and had its own lighting and telephone system, water supply, hospital and even cemetery. It was eventually captured on June 27 1917 by the French 164th division after desperate hand-to-hand fighting in total darkness. Visitors to the cavern have no need to duck their heads, for the ceiling is nowhere less than ten feet high. In one corner is a collection of uniforms, medals, newspapers of the day, rifles and machine guns. Other reminders of the grim battles fought along the ridge are the memorial chapel at Cerny, Hurtebise Farm, the trenches of the Casemates and the orientation table on the Plâteau de Californie near Craonne.

On the northern slopes of the crest topped by the *Chemin des Dames* is the forest of Vauclair (or Vauclerc), picturesque in its varying relief and contrasting foliage. In the Ailette valley at the edge of the forest is the ruined abbey of Vauclair, founded in 1134 on land donated by Barthelemy de Jur to his friend St Bernard, abbot of Clairvaux. The abbey was established by a group of monks headed by the Englishman Henry Murdoch, who later became the first abbot of Fountains in Yorkshire and in 1147 was made archbishop of York. Vauclair belonged to the order of Citeaux, created in the 12th century with the aim of observing the rule of St Benoit in all its primitive purity: obedience, silence, poverty, contemplation and charity. Recognisable among the ruins, which date from the 13th century when the monks rebuilt and improved the abbey, are the chapter, where the abbot read and interpreted a section of the bible, the cellar divided into two naves by a row of six columns, and the adjoining converts' refectory with a dormitory above. (Converts were lay brothers, mostly illiterate, who carried out menial tasks but like the monks took vows of chastity, poverty and obedience and to reciting every day the prayers they had learned by heart). The site is being excavated by students from Louvain university, their task being helped by the fact that all Cistercian monasteries were built to the same plan. Better perhaps than if they were still intact, the buildings illustrate the wonder of cross vaulting and other features of medieval construction in stone, including the use of cement based on lead as developed by the Romans. Near the ruins is the lake always attached to a monastery to provide the fish which formed the monks' staple diet.

In a vineyard three miles to the east is the ruined priory of Corbeny, said to have been linked to Vauclair by an underground passage. The abbey to which the priory belonged once housed the relics of St Marcoul, entrusted to Charles III in 898 by the monks of Nanteuil in the Côtentin fleeing from the Viking invaders. In the 5th century the saint had given to the French monarchs the power to heal the glandular swelling of the neck known as scrofula or king's evil (*le roi te touche, Dieu te guérisse*), Marcoul being derived from *mal* (pain) and *cou* (neck), and after being crowned many came to venerate the relics and to confirm that the ability to cure the disease had passed to them.

In medieval times the vineyards of Corbeny were noted for their wine but better known now is the mead produced in varying degrees of dryness to the extent of 700,000 bottles a year by the Caves à Hydromel Jorand. From its many beehives the modern *hydromellerie* collects the honey it uses to make the mead and also stages a fascinating exhibition devoted to the bees, which find no shortage of pollen in the fields of flowers surrounding the village.

Covering a lofty limestone plateau of varying relief west of Laon is the dense forest of St Gobain, crossed by an ancient Gallo-Roman road and pierced by sinuous valleys bordered in places by lakes. In the 7th century the Irish monk Gobain, who had come to evangelise the Laonnois, was martyred near the hermitage he had founded in the forest. The small town of St Gobain, which grew up round the hermit's sepulchre and the pilgrimage resulting from the miracles claimed to have been performed there, is also known for its *Manufacture des Glaces*, a glassworks established in 1665 by Colbert in Paris and transferred to its present location in 1692. The company began by making mirrors, examples of which are those in the *Salle des Glaces* in the palace of Versailles, and is now the world's third largest producer of glass. The narrow streets of the town converge on a Romanesque church built over a source of water said to have sprung from the staff of the saint.

The forest, much damaged in 1914-18 after being made an impregnable German stronghold with the Hindenburg Line running along its western edge, consists mostly of oak and beech trees — the largest of which is the Grosse Chêne, an oak 450 years old, 90 feet high and nearly 23 feet in circumference. Scenic roads traversing the forest, which still shelters many deer, lead to the ruins of several abbeys and other religious foundations. Two now on private property are the Benedictine abbey of St Nicolas aux Bois at the foot of

Abbey at Prémontré

an enclosed gorge and its former *dependance* le Tortoir, a 14th century fortified priory between two lakes. At the junction of seven valleys south of St Gobain is the mainly 12th century twin-towered church of Septvaux, with its primitive nave of the 11th century.

On the northern edge of the forest is the ancient village of Crépy en Laonnois, ringed by hills with names like Grosse Montagne, Mont Serval and Mont de Joie. The village formed part of the territory of Laon in 1643, though the villagers had obtained their own charter as early as 1184. Pillaged by the English under the Duke of Lancaster in the early 15th century, Crépy later witnessed the signing in its 13th century Notre Dame church on September 18 1544 of a treaty between François I and the Austrian Emperor Charles.

In the St Gobain forest the deer are hunted by horse and hound on Wednesdays and Saturdays from September to April, starting from Sinceny and Folembray on the west. There is no shortage of places to stay in the Laonnois but the oldest and nicest hostelry is the Bannière

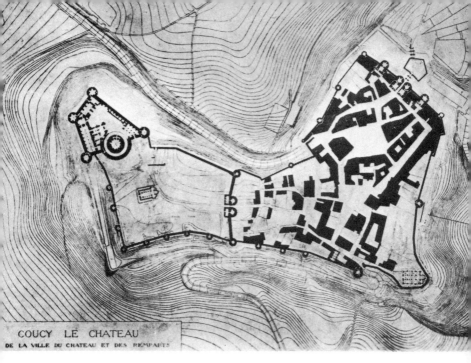

Plan of the Château, Coucy

de France at Laon, built in 1680 and tastefully modernised; it serves excellent food in a friendly atmosphere and has an extensive cellar.

The two religious orders most favoured in the diocese of Laon were the Premonstratensian and the Cistercian. Between the forests of St Gobain and Coucy is the former abbey of Premontré, founded in 1120 by St Norbert as the headquarters of a severe order of *chanoines regulières*, more priests than monks, who went out into the world preaching evangelism based on the lives of the apostles. The abbey buildings, restored in the 18th century, are now a psychiatric hospital, but visitors may enter the chapel facing the main entrance.

On the plain, the lower Coucy forest prolongs that of St Gobain on the west. Also damaged in the 1914-18 war, it is being replanted in many places with oak. In a clearing, the charming village of Barisis commands panoramic views of the Ailette valley. On an escarpment nearly 400 feet above the river is Coucy-le-Château, named after its famous castle, once the most formidable feudal fortress in Europe. It formed part of a fortified area, shaped like a "sleeping lion" occupying the top of the escarpment and ringed by ramparts punctuated by 28 towers which also enclosed the town and church and the *basse*

140

cour where the townsfolk sheltered in time of war. Built by Enguer-rand III in 1225 and incorporating great underground halls, the cas-tle was quadrangular in shape, with four great corner towers each 100 feet high. The keep, over 160 feet high and 100 feet in diameter, was blown up in the 1914-18 war by the occupying Germans, though the ruins still give a powerful impression of its role in feudal times.

The warlike lords of Coucy, each of whom proudly proclaimed "*Roy ne suis, ni prince ni comte aussi, je suis le sire de Coucy*", were indispensable allies of a feeble monarchy but subsequently became so powerful that they had to be cut down. Passionately fond of fight-ing and great Crusaders, they joined in many battles at the side of the king of France. Enguerrand VI was killed at the battle of Crécy in 1346. His successor Enguerrand VII, the last sire of Coucy, was cap-tured by the victorious English at the battle of Poitiers in 1356 and taken as a hostage to England, where he so charmed the astute Edward III that the king gave him his freedom, the hand of his daugh-ter Isabel and the county of Bedford as a dowry. After the death of Edward, Enguerrand left his wife and son in England and returned to France. Taken prisoner by the Turks while on a Crusade, he died in captivity at Bursa in 1397.

In the *ville haute* is the restored church of St Sauveur, the modern stained glass in which illustrates the story of Coucy, and in the town hall are frescoes depicting the powerful lords who governed it.

9
THE VALLEY OF THE MARNE

Among the last survivors of the vineyards that once covered much of Picardy are those on either side of Château-Thierry cloaking the north bank of the Marne, a broad and smiling river which swings in wild loops along a spacious valley past ancient villages backed by scenery that delights the eye.

Along the rim of the valley panoramic views are frequent, one of the highest vantage points on the west being that above the vineyards on the steep slopes of Mont Bonneil. East of Château-Thierry, where the views are no less extensive, the vines give way in places to farmland and woods. A pleasing change of scale is provided by the numerous streams flowing into the river from north and south. In and around the valley are some quaint villages to explore and several historic churches and châteaux to see; that there are not more is largely due to the bloody and destructive Battles of the Marne in 1914 and 1918.

Beyond the orientation table of Gland east of Château-Thierry, one of the prettiest villages beside the river is Mont St Père, from which scenic roads skirt Barbillon Wood to climb up to the hilltop hamlets of Epieds and Beuverines. From Epieds a road leads north to Fère-en-Tardenois and its impressive ruined 15th-century fortress crowning a tall earthwork approached by a high galleried viaduct across the deep moat surrounding it. Guardian of the approaches to the Ile de France and frequently under siege, it was transformed in the 16th century by Constable Anne de Montmorency: not a woman but a man and a great fighter into the bargain, who did his level best to unseat his arch enemy Catherine de Medici. The castle when occupied by the Germans in the Kaiser's war became one of the strong points in their Hindenburg Line.

Across the Marne from Château-Thierry is the charming early

Château of Condé en Brie

Gothic church and calvary of Mezy-Moulins, and upstream is the
bathing beach of Jaulgonne and the villages of Trelou and Passy,
two of the places where the still white wine of the valley, rarely seen
in Britain, is produced.

From Crezancy, on the left bank, a road along the pretty Surmelin
valley leads to the little 13th century church of St Eugene, where a
tympanum above the porch depicts in stone a symbolic representa-
tion of the Last Judgement — with the Devil claiming those souls
found to be too heavy when placed on a pair of scales. A few miles on
is the vast château of Condé-en-Brie, built by Enguerrand de Coucy
in the early 12th century and altered several times since. The château
was inherited in 1518 by Louis de Bourbon, who took its name when
he assumed the title of prince of Condé, but it is now owned by the de
Sade family. It was bequeathed to them in 1814 and is still their
home. The present Comte de Sade, who had the job of rehabilitating
the château, has added documents and jewellery of the period to the
decorations and furnishings, little altered since they were installed
two centuries ago. These include a music room decorated with
murals by the Italian architect Servandoni, paintings by Watteau,

Oudry and others and specially-designed furniture signed by the
18th century craftsmen by whom it was made. Visitors can see the
table on which Molière wrote and the bed in which Cardinal Richelieu slept, as well as records of the ownership of the château and letters written by the count's notorious ancestor the Marquis de Sade
while serving his 28-year prison sentence.

South of the château is the village of Pargny la Dhuys, where the
waters of the Dhuys are collected and carried by aqueduct to emerge
from the taps of Parisiens sixty miles away.

Château — Thierry

On view in the château of Condé en Brie is a painting by the French artist Lancret illustrating one of the famous fables of Jean de la Fontaine, who was born and lived most of his life at Château-Thierry, a small Gallo-Roman settlement when in 718 Charles Martel built a castle there for the Merovingian king Thierry V, from whom the town subsequently took its name. Enlarged and fortified in the 11th and 12th centuries, the castle was taken by the English during the Hundred Years' War and the ruins dominating the old town on the north bank of the Marne now enclose a public garden from which there are wide views of the valley. Still standing in the ramparts are the fortified gates of St Jean and St Pierre. Among the narrow streets of the ancient quarter on the same side of the river is the house where la Fontaine lived in the 17th century, now converted to a museum containing paintings, drawings and engravings illustrating his life and work. At the age of 37 he became, like his father before him, the local master of waters and forests, employment which gave him ample opportunity to study the animals, birds and insects he features with such inimitable irony in his fables.

On a height above the river south of Château Thierry is the village of Nesles la Montagne, the scene in 1814 of a battle in which the French defeated the Russians. From nearby Luberon farm, which Napoleon made his headquarters during the fighting, there are views of the battlefield. Monuments to the northeast commemorating later battles, in which the Americans fought by the side of the French in 1918, are at Côte 204 and, beyond, at Bois Belleau, a village dominated by a hill on which are American and German military cemeteries and some of the dugouts and trenches used during the conflict.

One of the most picturesque places in the western section of the Marne is Chezy, on the left bank of the river and with a notable abbey church. Through the village flows the Dolloir stream, the waters of which serve the ancient *lavoir* — replaced in most households now by a washing machine. Beside the upper reaches of the Dolloir is the Romanesque parish church of Essises, remarkable in its austerity.

From Azy, which faces Chezy across the Marne, a road climbs up through the vineyards to Mont Bonneil. Downstream, curiously named Charly is a typical Marne wine village at the mouth of the Gousset valley. There are fine views from Crouttes, on the same side of the river and also engaged in producing wine from the vineyards that surround it. Nogent l'Artaud, on the left bank of the Marne, is an ancient small town which owes part of its name to the rich treasurer of the duchy of Champagne, who built a castle there in 1158 on becoming the local seigneur. Nogent has an interesting church, in

145

Côte 204 American War Memorial, Château-Thierry

which the choir and baptismal fonts are of the 12th century and the nave of the 16th; inside is the 12th century tomb of the fifth son of Artaud. Nearby are the ruins of the convent of Clarisses, founded by Blanche of Champagne in 1299. It is a pleasant drive south from Nogent to the pretty forest-ringed Vergis lake.

The valley is a scene of great activity when the grapes are harvested in the autumn. It is then, when the crop has been safely gathered in, that the Marnois are at their most hospitable. Reserved but good humoured, they are orientated more to good conversation than to the pleasures of the table, though with the clean-tasting local wine and the rich produce from the district to go with it, these are by no means lacking.

*　　*　　*

Long after their empire crumbled the eight great roads built by the Romans for the defence of northern Gaul were still there to ease the path of the invader. One of these, which echoed to the march of foreign armies more than any other, cuts like a knife through the heart of the Thiérache.

In this geologically-distinct region, north of the plain centred on Laon, where the clay subsoil creates a moist climate to promote the growth of all things green, the rolling landscape of rich meadows, orchards and woods conceals many an ancient village and isolated farm tucked away in narrow pastoral valleys. Travellers who leave

Fortified church at Prisces in the Thiérache

the Roman highway to follow one of the valley roads turn a corner to be suddenly confronted by what appears to be a castle — a closer look reveals it is neither castle nor church but a combination of both.

Over fifty rustic villages in the Thiérache shelter beneath a fortified church displaying all the features of a medieval fortress ready to withstand a siege. The churches are simple, austere even, with none of the ornate decoration found elsewhere. The big difference is that people built them not out of local pride but to protect their own lives and their few possessions against the bloodthirsty mercenaires and outlaws who roamed the region in the long misery of the 16th and 17th centuries, when the Thiérache formed the northernmost part of France and the villagers' only refuge was in their place of worship.

Evangelised in the 7th and 8th centuries by Irish monks led by St Algis, a disciple of St Columban, the Thiérache seems to have reverted to semi-paganism after the invasions of the Normans and the uncertain rule of the Carolingian kings. By the 12th century a second evangelical campaign became necessary. Encouraged by the bishop of Laon, St Norbert, founder of the order of Premontré, established abbeys at many places in the region, the monks undertaking the task of reconverting the peasants to Christianity. To ensure the survival of religious belief, the abbeys promoted the construction of parish churches by providing the money for the white stone used to build them. The result was a flowering of religious architecture throughout the Thiérache in the 12th and 13th centuries.

From the 12th to the 15th century the region prospered, despite invasions by the Flemish and the English in the 14th century, from whom the villagers protected themselves — if not their crops — by fortifying the walls enclosing the cemetery, here around the church and not at the edge of the village as in other parts of France. But for most of the 16th and 17th centuries the Thiérache was cast in the role of frontier region, with the Hainault a few miles north across what is now the Belgian border occupied by Austrian and Spanish armies constantly at war with the king of France, each side fighting for the control of strategic roads and towns and in the process devastating the surrounding countryside. Yet troops on the move were perhaps less to be feared than those who stayed put — like the merceneries in the pay of the marshal of France who arrived in 1646 and spent much of their time looting and burning villages, often on the orders of their officers. Those peasants who could escaped with the few possessions they had — a cart pulled by a pair of lean horses, a bed, a cooking pot and perhaps a cow — only to be refused entry to towns where they sought sanctuary and, if they survived, condemned to live by force like those from whom they had fled. Some French officers ordered their troops to steal crops on a commercial scale, selling the produce in the markets at Laon, Vervins and elsewhere. Why? Because, and this was not uncommon in those days, no food was supplied to them as of right. They were simply expected to find their own where they could.

The idea of erecting a defensive wall round their churchyard no doubt led the villagers to fortify the church itself, the size of the fortifications depending upon their numbers and resources. Using bricks made of clay dug and fired on the spot, they built a massive keep above the porch or the choir, often truly formidable and sometimes linked to underground shelters. They also built round towers, either in place of or in addition to a keep. Aptly-named *meurtrieres* or loopholes were set in both keep and towers, some at the height of a man, for the villagers intended to be active in their own defence. Some fortified areas contain a well, a bread oven and a fireplace for cooking meals. In times of danger, the windows of the unfortified part of the church were also bricked up.

Brick was also the material used in 1549 to fortify the castle of François de Guise on a hill overlooking the small town of Guise in the Oise valley, on the western edge of the Thiérache. The fresh colour of the red brick fortifications, most of them below ground and consisting of several interlinked systems of defence, contrasts sharply with the dull sandstone of the original 13th century fortress. The superstructure, which included a *basse cour* where the peasants and their animals sheltered in time of war, was shelled by German artillery in 1914-18, leaving only the keep intact. The ruins are being excavated voluntarily by students of all nationalities who have already revealed the foundations of two churches and some of the many underground halls and passages, among them a spacious guardroom and a food store. Some historians believe that the underground defences include tunnels which link the castle, capable of accommodating a force of 7,000 men, with the fortified churches of the Thiérache, of which they say Guise formed the military capital. This suggests that the churches were part of an overall plan of defence, a theory apparently disproved by the fact that many were fortified, or their fortifications restored or enlarged, at widely different times. Yet since the invaders came mostly from the northeast Guise was a vital bastion guarding the route to Paris and the churches may well have served as forward outposts.

The principal rivers and streams in the Thiérache flow from east to west across the region, but neither they nor their valleys put up any real obstacle to the invader. Yet it is in the valleys that settlements are most numerous. The northernmost river is the upper Oise, which

149

Church at Beaurain near Guise

rises near Hirson and ends at its junction with the Sambre-Oise canal
beyond Guise. South of Vervins is the Brune stream and below that
the Serre, which links Rozoy, Montcornet and Marle and marks the
southern limit of the region.

One of the most impressive churches in the Oise valley is Beaurain,
on a height between two villages east of Guise. Round towers flank
both choir and nave, above which are rooms in which the people of
the two villages found shelter. The church at Macquiny, beside the
river west of Guise, displays an imposing keep with a stone above the
portal bearing the date — 1501 — when it was fortified. Unusually,
the choir is higher than the nave and the towers are decorated with
arcades. At Audigny southwest of Beaurain is a fortified farm typical
of many which once existed in the Thiérache.

In a pretty location above the river, the church at Englancourt has a square keep flanked by two towers and a choir with a flat roof which reinforces two other circular towers. A winding staircase within the walls leads to a vast refuge. Nearby St Algis, its fortifications forming a massive rectangle built or restored in 1634, has rooms in the upper part of the keep measuring 22 feet square reached by stairs little wider than a man and thereby easier to defend against intruders. A not uncommon feature are the glazed bricks laid in geometric patterns in the walls.

A pleasant small town noted for its fishing, Etreaupont stands at the confluence of the Oise and its tributary the Thon. In the pretty Thon valley to the east are the historic ruins of the abbey of Foigny, founded in 1121 by Barthelemy de Jur, bishop of Laon. This indefatigable ecclesiastic also founded the abbeys of Boheries near Guise, Thenailles near Vervins, Clairfontaine near La Capelle and the chartreuse of Val St Pierre south of the Brune, all of which are now in ruins. Etreaupont is linked with La Capelle on the north by the old Roman highway running vertically through the Thiérache. Between the two towns is the fortified church of Lerzy, restored in 1630 and frequently under attack since the village was one of the first human habitations near the road down which most of the invading merceneries came.

*   *   *

La Capelle, a small town at the junction of five main roads, is famous on three counts. For its age-old cheese fair staged in early September, when you can taste the savoury local Rollot and Maroilles cheeses, the second perhaps in a stronger version matured in beer called Vieux Lille; for its horse races and horse breeding; and of course because it was the place where the German envoys on the way to sign the Armistice crossed the French lines on 7 November 1918. After they had been escorted across Northern France to a château near Compiègne the Allied troops continued their advance towards Germany. The Kaiser's war did little damage to the Thiérache. Another change on this occasion was that the foreigners making their way across the region were not demanding war but asking for peace.

Along the Oise valley east of Etreaupont is the church of Wimy, its huge keep flanked by enormous round towers still indented with bullet holes. Inside the porch are two big fireplaces and a well, with a large refuge above.

The church at Vervins, an animated small hilltop town on the main road south of Etreaupont which was an administrative centre in Gallo-Roman times, is unusual in being fortified from within and possesses neither towers nor keep. The church was first protected in the 14th century by fortifying the walls of the cemetery around it. The formerly fortified town is centred on a *hôtel de ville* where on 2 May 1598 was signed the treaty by which Philip II of Spain recognised Henri IV as king of France. Northeast to Vervins, the church at La Bouteille — built by the monks of Foigny in 1547 — is the only one in the region constructed at the outset as a fortress.

The prettiest valley in the Thiérache and the one with some of the most interesting churches is the Brune, a short way south. The most important church is undoubtedly Prisces. Above the porch is a huge square keep for four storeys and 80 feet high flanked by diagonally opposed towers which could accommodate a hundred men for a week with their food and arms. Above the nave is the refuge for the villagers. Equally intriguing though smaller is its counterpart at Burelles, incorporating many defensive elements. A circular staircase in one of the towers adjoining the keep leads to a large hall on the first floor designated *salle de garde*, with a vaulted brick rood and a fireplace, and above it another chamber labelled *salle des juifs* and used as both a refuge and a prison. The adjoining parish of Hary, was in the 12th century owned by the abbey of Ste Corneille of Compiègne and under the protection of the sires of Coucy, seigneurs of Vervins, has a fortified church with walls nearly five feet thick.

Along the Huteau, which flows into the Brune near Hary, is the spectacular façade of the imposing church of Plomion; hundreds of people could shelter in the roof space extending above the nave from the transept to the choir. From the ground floor of the keep a narrow passage leads to a prison in which were confined both captured attackers and local criminals. The square-towered church at nearby Jeantes, containing 10th century baptismal fonts and expressionist stained glass and frescoes by the Dutch artist Charles Eyck, has a rectangular keep in front of the nave. The tower on the left, entered by steps from outside, served for many years as the *mairie*.

Beside the upper reaches of the Brune south of the Huteau is the village of Dagny, where a fortified farm has a dovecot above the entrance to its inner courtyard. At Cuiry les Iviers not far away the church has some curious fortifications: two large towers are placed diagonally, one left of the porch, the other to the right of the altar, to the left of which is a smaller tower.

At Dohis the church is virtually all porch and keep and is enclosed by a high cemetery wall. The building, one of the first to be fortified, dates from the time of the Hundred Years' War. Prettily located near the source of the Brune nearby is the pleasant small town of Brune-hamel, at an altitude of 830ft one of the highest points in the Thiér-ache. Centred on an immense square, it is the scene of an age-old market in wheat and barley.

Between Brunehamel and the Serre valley to the south are the churches of Parfondval and Archon, the first approached through a fortified gateway, the second with a porch flanked by two round towers linked by a sentry walk.

One of the most ambient places in the Serre valley is Rozoy, where the townsfolk show their keenness for European unity by acting as hosts to groups of visitors of all nationalities.

The vast and severely styled St Martin church at Montcornet, its choir, nave and transept dating from the 13th century, has a fine Renaissance portal and 16th century fortifications made up of no less than eight round towers, in each of which are loopholes at the height of a man from which crossbows could be fired at attackers. Underground passages link the church with the town square and in their choir are wood carvings from the abbey of Val St Pierre, the ruins of which stand at the edge of the Bois du Val a few miles to the north. In the early middle ages the town was populated mostly by Jewish merchants, many of whom emigrated in the 14th century. It was at Montcornet, at the junction of two Roman roads, that General (then colonel) de Gaulle's unit of 120 tanks, with enough petrol for only five hours' running, tried to slow down the German armoured divisions commanded by Guderian on May 15, 1940. The town was almost deserted and had been extensively damaged by the bombing the night before of two munitions trains standing at the station.

The Hurtaut stream flows northwest to join the Serre at Montcornet; along the valley are fortified farms built on the traditional Picard pattern of a square enclosing an open courtyard, two examples of which are at Montloue and Berlise.

The Serre flows past the fortified churches of Chaourse, Tavaux and Bosmont to enter Marle, on a spur above the valley. The church at Bosmont has a large keep built on one side of the nave and balanced on the other by a chapel; inside the keep is an inscription relating the success of the catholics over the protestants at the first stirrings of the Reformation. The ancient small town of Marle, with its 13th century church housing the tomb of a local noble and behind it the courtyard of a ruined castle forming a terrace above the river, was mentioned in the Treaty of Verdun of 843 and still fills an age-long function as a rural market.

That the churches needed to be fortified as far south as the Serre indicates how deeply the invaders penetrated. Nowhere in the region were people safe. It was not until new territory was ceded to France by the Treaty of the Pyrenees in 1659 that the Thiérache ceased to be a frontier region. Only then could the long suffering and hard working people live in peace and welcome rather than suspect the stranger, and here, on the final frontier of France let us leave them.

TRAVEL INFORMATION

Picardy and Artois lie directly across the Channel from the coast of Kent, and are the nearest French provinces to the United Kingdom. Artois is now embraced by the region of Nord de France, while Picardy, by far the larger province, still retains its antique identity.

MAPS

The Michelin 'Red' maps are ideal for selecting a route, and the Northern section gives an adequate scale. Once you arrive in France it is advisable to buy the Institut Géographique National Carte Touristique, scale 1:25,000 which shows all the ancient and historic sites, and is also easy to follow.

TOURIST INFORMATION

The French Government Tourist Office at 178 Piccadilly, London SW1 will supply all the available brochures and hotel information you require.

Ask for information on Picardy and Nord de France (for Artois). Each town in France has its own Information Bureau, or *Syndicate d'Initiative*, and a visit there on arrival to obtain more detailed local information is well worth while.

GUIDE BOOKS

Three indispensable guides for the traveller in France are the *Michelin* 'Red' *Guide*, the *Guide des Relais Routiers*, and the *Guide des Logis de France et Auberges Rurales*. The latter, better known simply as '*The Logis*', lists some 4,000 family-owned hotels in provincial France, which usually offer excellent food and comfortable accommodation. The '*Relais Routier*' lists cafés and small restaurants patronized by the French lorry drivers, where food is often good and always plentiful.

While you can pay ruinous prices for food and accommodation in France, by and large you will find that you are offered good food, at reasonable prices, which together offer excellent value for money.

To these three basic tools, the enthusiastic visitor could add the Michelin Green Guide '*Nord de la France*', and if you speak a little French, the gastronomic guide known as the *Gault-Millau*. If you wish to find a holiday flat or cottage in the country then the Gîtes de France organization will have something to offer you, and their accommodation can now be booked in England at the Tourist Office in Piccadilly; details are published annually in '*The French Farm and Village Holiday Guide*', distributed by Mitchell-Beazley.

HOTELS AND RESTAURANTS

The Michelin and Gault-Millau guides give lots of information on where to stay and eat, but the following would be worth visiting.

Albert: Hotel de la Basillique.

Amiens: Le Godbert Restaurant, much patronized during the 1914-18 war by such poets as Sassoon and Robert Graves, still excellent.

Ardres: The Hotel et Restaurant Grand Clement.

Arras: Hotel Grandes Arcades.

Beaurains: Le Chanzy Restaurant, or L'Auberge.

Béthune: Hotel Bernard et de la Gare.

Calais: Hotel Meurice.

Le Crotoy: Hotel de la Baie, Chez Mado.

Dury: La Bonne Auberge.

Wimereux: Hotel et Restaurant L'Atlantic.

INDEX

158